$22.95

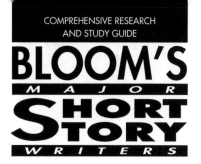

COMPREHENSIVE RESEARCH
AND STUDY GUIDE

# BLOOM'S
## MAJOR
# SHORT
# STORY
## WRITERS

*Nikolai*

*Gogol*

EDITED AND WITH AN
INTRODUCTION BY HAROLD BLOOM

# CURRENTLY AVAILABLE

COMPREHENSIVE RESEARCH
AND STUDY GUIDE

BLOOM'S
*MAJOR*
SHORT
STORY
*WRITERS*

# Nikolai Gogol

CHELSEA HOUSE
PUBLISHERS
A Haights Cross Communications Company

Philadelphia

First Printing
1 3 5 7 9 8 6 4 2

Library of Congress Cataloging-in-Publication Data

Nikolai Gogol / edited and with an introduction by Harold Bloom.
       p. cm. — (Bloom's Major Short Story Writers)
Includes bibliographical references and index.
   ISBN 0-7910-7588-5
   1. Gogol, Nikolai Vasilevich, 1809–1852—Criticism and
interpretation. 2. Gogol, Nikolai Vasilevich, 1809–1852—Examinations—
Study guides. I. Bloom, Harold. II. Title. III. Series.
   PG3335.Z8N59 2003
   891.78'309—dc22

                                                            2003016872


Chelsea House Publishers
1974 Sproul Road, Suite 400
Broomall, PA 19008-0914

www.chelseahouse.com


Contributing Editor: Jennifer Vogel

Cover design by Keith Trego

Layout by EJB Publishing Services

# CONTENTS

# USER'S GUIDE

This volume is designed to present biographical, critical, and bibliographical information on the author and the author's best-known or most important short stories. Following Harold Bloom's editor's note and introduction is a concise biography of the author that discusses major life events and important literary accomplishments. A critical analysis of each story follows, tracing significant themes, patterns, and motifs in the work. An annotated list of characters supplies brief information on the main characters in each story.

A selection of critical extracts, derived from previously published material, follows each thematic analysis. In most cases, these extracts represent the best analysis available from a number of leading critics. Because these extracts are derived from previously published material, they will include the original notations and references when available. Each extract is cited, and readers are encouraged to use the original publications as they continue their research. A bibliography of the author's writings, a list of additional books and articles on the author and their work, and an index of themes and ideas conclude the volume.

As with any study guide, this volume is designed as a supplement to the works being discussed, and is in no way intended as a replacement for those works. The reader is advised to read the text prior to using this study guide, and to keep it accessible for quick reference.

# ABOUT THE EDITOR

**Harold Bloom** is Sterling Professor of the Humanities at Yale University and Henry W. and Albert A. Berg Professor of English at the New York University Graduate School. He is the author of over 20 books, and the editor of more than 30 anthologies of literary criticism.

Professor Bloom's works include *Shelley's Mythmaking* (1959), *The Visionary Company* (1961), *Blake's Apocalypse* (1963), *Yeats* (1970), *A Map of Misreading* (1975), *Kabbalah and Criticism* (1975), *Agon: Toward a Theory of Revisionism* (1982), *The American Religion* (1992), *The Western Canon* (1994), and *Omens of Millennium: The Gnosis of Angels, Dreams, and Resurrection* (1996). *The Anxiety of Influence* (1973) sets forth Professor Bloom's provocative theory of the literary relationships between the great writers and their predecessors. His most recent books include *Shakespeare: The Invention of the Human*, a 1998 National Book Award finalist, *How to Read and Why* (2000), *Genius: A Mosaic of One Hundred Exemplary Creative Minds* (2002), and *Hamlet: Poem Unlimited* (2003).

Professor Bloom earned his Ph.D. from Yale University in 1955 and has served on the Yale faculty since then. He is a 1985 MacArthur Foundation Award recipient and served as the Charles Eliot Norton Professor of Poetry at Harvard University in 1987–88. In 1999 he was awarded the prestigious American Academy of Arts and Letters Gold Medal for Criticism. Professor Bloom is the editor of several other Chelsea House series in literary criticism, including BLOOM'S MAJOR SHORT STORY WRITERS, BLOOM'S MAJOR NOVELISTS, BLOOM'S MAJOR DRAMATISTS, BLOOM'S MODERN CRITICAL INTERPRETATIONS, BLOOM'S MODERN CRITICAL VIEWS, and BLOOM'S BIOCRITIQUES.

# EDITOR'S NOTE

My Introduction sneaks up on the marvelous (and mad) Gogol, by interpreting the grand story, "Gogol's Wife" by the modern Italian disciple of Gogol, Tommaso Landolfi. In my judgment, "Gogol's Wife" is one of the best interpretations available of Gogol's highly original mode of fantasy.

As there are twenty-three critical views presented here, in regard to five stories, I will comment upon only a representative handful.

"The Portrait" is read by Donald Fanger as Gogol's quest for an aesthetic transcendence, while Derek Maus explores the daemonic in the story.

Leonard J. Kent, in a strong paragraph, introduces the theme of doubles as central to "Nevsky Prospect," after which the uncanny and hilarious "The Nose" is allegorized by David McDuff as Gogol's indictment of moral blindness.

"The Overcoat," most influential of Gogolian tales, is seen by Simon Karlinsky as the epitome of urban alienation, while James B. Woodward charts the shapes of sexual nightmare in "Ivan Shponka and His Aunt."

# Harold Bloom

Dostoevsky famously said: "We all came out from under Gogol's 'Overcoat,'" a short story concerning a wretched copying clerk whose new overcoat is stolen. Disdained by the authorities, to whom he duly protests, the poor fellow dies, after which his ghost continues to search vainly for justice. Good as the story is, it is not the best of Gogol, which may be "Old-World Landowners" or the insane "The Nose," which begins when a barber, at breakfast, discovers a customer's nose inside a loaf of bread freshly baked by his wife. The spirit of Gogol, subtly alive in much of Nabokov, achieves its apotheosis in the triumphant "Gogol's Wife," by the modern Italian story-writer Tommaso Landolfi, perhaps the funniest and most unnerving story that I've yet read.

The narrator, Gogol's friend and biographer, "reluctantly" tells us the story of Gogol's wife. The actual Gogol, a religious obsessive, never married, and deliberately starved himself to death at forty-three or so, after burning his unpublished manuscripts. But Landolfi's Gogol (who might have been invented by Kafka or by Borges) has married a rubber balloon, a splendidly inflatable dummy who assumes different shapes and sizes at her husband's whim. Much in love with his wife, in one of her forms or another, Gogol enjoys sexual relations with her, and bestows upon her the name Caracas, after the capital of Venezuela, for reasons known only to the mad writer.

For some years, all goes well, until Gogol contracts syphilis, which he rather unfairly blames upon Caracas. Ambivalence towards his silent wife gains steadily in Gogol through the years. He accuses Caracas of self-gratification, and even betrayal, so that she becomes bitter and excessively religious. Finally, the enraged Gogol pumps too much air into Caracas (quite deliberately) until she bursts and scatters into the air. Collecting the remnants of Madame Gogol, the great writer burns them in the fireplace, where they share the fate of his unpublished works. Into the same fire, Gogol casts also a rubber doll, the son of

Caracas. After this final catastrophe, the biographer defends Gogol from the charge of wife-beating, and salutes the memory of the writer's lofty genius.

The best prelude (or postlude) to reading Landolfi's "Gogol's Wife" is to read some stories by Gogol, on the basis of which we will not doubt the reality of the unfortunate Caracas. She is as likely a paramour as Gogol could ever have discovered (or invented) for himself. In contrast, Landolfi could hardly have composed much the same story and called it "Maupassant's Wife," let alone "Turgenev's Wife." No, it has to be Gogol and Gogol alone, and I rarely doubt Landolfi's story, particularly just after each rereading. Caracas has a reality that Borges neither seeks nor achieves for his Tlön. As Gogol's only possible bride, she seems to me the ultimate parody of Frank O'Connor's insistence that the lonely voice crying out in the modern short story is that of the Submerged Population. Who could be more submerged than Gogol's wife?

—Originally published in *How to Read and Why?* New York: Scribner, 2000: 60–62.

# Nikolai Gogol

For his short life and even shorter career, Nikolai Gogol was a remarkably prolific writer. His creative output is also impressive for its diversity in various genres. Gogol wrote poems, plays, novels, short stories, essays, and tracts, with varying degrees of success in each. And within each genre, Gogol was adept at dealing with a variety of topics and subjects. For example, his short stories move from the Ukrainian countryside to the affairs of cosmopolitan St. Petersburg with equal skill; furthermore, his collection *Arabesques* is comprised of essays that discuss art, history, poetry, and even geography.

Gogol continues to resist definitive interpretation—words used to describe him and his work have included "elusiveness," "enigma," "riddle." At the same time, however, his work is able to conform to a variety of differing interpretations. Each school of criticism claimed—and continues to claim—Gogol for its own purposes. The Romantics, Realists, Symbolists, Formalists, Structuralists, and others interpret his writings' relevance to their respective school of thought. Gogol held a particular fascination for Russian literary critics. In fact, it has been said that a history of nineteenth- and twentieth-century Russian criticism could effectively focus solely on the readings of Gogol's texts. It seems that contemporary critics have become resigned to the diversity of interpretations that are possible and view his work in a more relativistic state of mind than that of their predecessors. And even earlier than the present critics, Nabokov wrote an essay that attempted to expose the absurdity of trying to pigeonhole Gogol into any social or political category. Indeed, Gogol's work continues to resist all labels; it is truly original.

Nikolai Vasilievich Gogol was born March 20, 1809 (April 1 in the Gregorian calendar)[1] in the small Ukrainian town of Sorochintsy to Vasily Afanasyevich Gogol-Yanovsky and Marya Ivanovna, née Kosyarovsky. His parents belonged to the petty landed gentry and their ancestors were of Cossack origin. The second part of the family name, which Gogol later dropped, hints at connections with Polish aristocracy. His mother was an acutely neurotic woman who married at fourteen and had a total of five children, two boys and three girls, Gogol being the eldest. His father seems to have held no definite occupation, but had artistic interests and wrote comedies in Ukrainian for private performances in the mansions of the local gentry. He died in 1825 when Gogol was sixteen and attending high school.

In 1821, at age twelve, Gogol was sent to a boarding school at Nezhin where he remained for seven years. In 1828, he moved to St. Petersburg, the capital. He found work in the city as a civil servant in the department of public buildings of the Ministry of the Interior. Although he did not last long in this position, it provided material for his later fiction.

While in St. Petersburg, Gogol took a pair of teaching positions in which he could exercise his strong interest in history. In 1831, he became a professor at the Patriotic Institute, a school for girls, and in 1834, he was appointed assistant professor of history at St. Petersburg University. Concurrent with these positions, he was becoming an established writer with a developing reputation.

But before this success, his first work, a narrative poem entitled *Hans Küechelgarten* (1829), which he published under a pseudonym, was universally savaged by critics. He then switched to prose fiction, and began to write stories of Ukrainian life. In 1831 and 1832 Gogol published a two-volume collection entitled *Evenings on a Farm Near Dikanka*. In 1835, he put out two new volumes of stories: *Arabesques* and *Mirgorod*. These collections, as well as the play *The Inspector General* a year later, established him as a major Russian writer. Vissarion Belinsky, beginning his career as a critic, even ranked him beside Alexander Pushkin.

These two figures, Belinsky and Pushkin, ended up playing crucial roles in Gogol's successful career as a writer. In 1831, Gogol met the prose writer and dramatist Pushkin, an individual who would have the most influence of any person on his creative output. The relationship was not simply one-sided but symbiotic, for in 1836 when Pushkin launched his quarterly, *The Contemporary*, Gogol was one of its principal contributors. Belinsky, Russia's most important nineteenth-century critic, is frequently imputed with initiating Gogol's literary career. His "Literary Reveries" (1834) and the essay "On the Russian Story and the Stories of Mr. Gogol" (1835) both established him as a major literary critic and introduced Gogol to the reading public. He argued that Gogol was the most truthful of Russian writers, the first one to have shown Russian life as it really was.

Gogol was particularly able to vividly depict the world of St. Petersburg, a city that had an enormous impact on him. This city plays a paramount role in three of the stories in *Arabesques* and in a number of uncollected stories that Gogol wrote over the next seven years, from 1835–1842. In fact, St. Petersburg is such a focal point in these particular stories, that they have been labeled, in an informal grouping, as the "Petersburg Tales." These stories of urban life, bureaucracy, and alienation form stark contrasts to those of the *Dikanka* collection, which feature simple peasants and rustic Ukrainian life, images from Gogol's earlier life.

Gogol did not just move between different regions of Russia, he also traveled outside of its borders a great deal. His peripatetic nature was motivated, in part, by his general dissatisfaction with life and the reception of some of his works. After critics ridiculed his play *The Inspector General*, and he himself was disappointed by both the St. Petersburg and the Moscow productions, Gogol went abroad. There he remained, mostly in Rome, from 1836 until 1848, returning to Russia only twice during that time. It was in Rome, a place that he truly loved, where he felt more at home than he did anywhere else.

In Rome, he began *Dead Souls*, the most ambitious undertaking of his career, a work which he conceived as becoming a new *Divine Comedy*. Part I was published in 1842 to great critical acclaim; however, Part II did not advance to Gogol's satisfaction, and he destroyed the various manuscripts for it three times.

Gogol's goal had always been to transform the baseness of reality that he depicted in his art and simultaneously bring about the spiritual regeneration of his readers, but during the 1840s, the notion of his art having a semi-divine mission took on an added urgency. During this period, he became more and more preoccupied with the search for religious truths and self-perfection, which he documented in his extensive letter-writing, and which he tried to express definitively in *Selected Passages from a Correspondence with Friends* (1847). This work, constructed as a series of letters, came to be seen by Gogol as the most important statement of his life; however, neither public nor critical reception supported this notion.

In this composition, his most controversial publication, Gogol produced a work that was out of touch with the sensibilities of the age. His goal was to strengthen and preserve Russian society as it was, complete with serfs, and the extremely reactionary publication received angry responses from both his friends and his enemies. The work prompted Belinsky, formerly Gogol's biggest supporter, to write his vitriolic "Letter to Gogol," a ten-page letter excoriating Gogol for his beliefs. In it, he asserted that Gogol had understood neither the spirit nor the form of modern Christianity.

Gogol, hurting from Belinsky's criticism and feeling as if he needed to undergo religious penance, went on a pilgrimage to the Holy Land in 1848. This trip failed to bring the spiritual reinvigoration he had hoped for, and in 1851, he returned to Russia where he settled in Moscow until his death a year later.

Gogol's agonizing death, in some ways, reflected his life, a life filled with both physical and mental suffering, with these two categories often blending together. He suffered from a number of physical ailments, the most noted being a stomach ailment which caused or was caused by serious emotional depression. He was also a hypochondriac, and had traveled from one European spa to another. His death on February 21 (March 4 in the Gregorian calendar), 1852, at the age of forty-three, was largely from self-inflicted malnutrition and general debilitation.

NOTE

1. There was a switch in 1918 in Russia from the Julian to the Gregorian calendar, which is eleven days later.

# "The Portrait"

"The Portrait" was originally published in Part I of *Arabesques* in 1835, but it was later revised and republished in 1842 in *The Contemporary*. "The Portrait" is actually comprised of two stories, each of them more or less complete in and of themselves; what links them is the portrait in question. The first section tells the story of an artist whose ruin is induced by a recently acquired portrait of a moneylender. The second section details how the portrait came to be painted and its evil origins, a story that is imbedded ingeniously within another plot thread that takes place in an auction.

The title of the story suggests that the story is a portrait of Chartkov, the main character of the first story, an artist who gives up his talent, and in pandering to the public and in his quest for gold, becomes as shallow as the people he paints and as flat as the canvas on which he paints them. Although he is a struggling artist, he has a promising talent, but according to his professor, is impatient. The same professor warns him against painting in a fashionable manner, and says that already he sees him being enticed by worldly possessions. This will ruin talent, he cautions him, and the scene is set for the narrative, detailing Chartkov's downfall, that will unfold. It is important to note that the seeds of Chartkov's ruin are already sown within himself; it is not entirely the corrupting force of an outside influence—the portrait's money—that leads to his destruction.

Although "The Portrait" is a warning against obsession with materialism, it is also about art and the proper role of the artist. It speaks to the necessity of finding a balance between hyperrealism (the portrait) and excessive craft to the point of falsity (Chartkov's society portraits). The story shows that the artist's true calling is not to recollect reality (*anamnesis*), nor to copy it (*mimesis*), but rather to reveal what is hidden in it (*aletheia*). That is, the role of the artist is one of creator rather than copier of nature, and it is his job to reveal the inscrutable idea that is concealed in everything. The story emphasizes the artist's soul as the refiner and purifier of reality. The them of

"The Portrait" can also be considered in light of both Gogol's devout Christianity and perhaps his own questioning of his career as a practitioner of another type of art: writing.

## PART I

"The Portrait" begins with Chartkov visiting a shop that sells paintings. He shakes his head at the vulgarity of the common taste in art. The owner tries to get him to buy a painting, but Chartkov is unmoved by what he considers to be rubbish. But then his eye catches on a portrait of an old man, garbed in an Asiatic costume, and he is riveted. The eyes of the subject, especially, transfix him with their uncanny animation. The twenty kopecks he spends on the portrait are his last, but he feels as if he has had no choice in the matter—the painting has begun to control him.

Chartkov returns to his studio to the news, reported by his assistant Nikita, that the landlord and a policeman have paid a visit with promises of evicting him if the rent is not paid when they return the next day. Chartkov is often frustrated when he sees someone, sometimes not even a professional artist, amassing a fortune by catering to popular tastes. He is immune to such frustrations, however, when he is immersed completely in his work. But now, with impending eviction, he laments this situation, feeling as if his life's work has hitherto been worthless.

All of a sudden Chartkov shudders, frightened by the face of the recently acquired portrait. The feeling soon subsides and he sets about cleaning it and is again struck by the vitality of the eyes. Chartkov is reminded of the story of a portrait by Leonardo da Vinci in which the eyes seem similarly to be strangely human. In this case, though, he is struck by the notion that the representation of the eyes is not art; it even destroys the harmony of the portrait. He ponders why such a realistic depiction of the man's features would provoke such anguished feelings in himself, wondering whether it is precisely this literalism that unnerves him and seems removed from the realm of transformative art. To him, the eyes do not seem to be copies from nature but actual eyes ripped from a human face. The position that mere imitation is not art is a theme that is emphasized throughout the story.

The portrait, and these eyes especially, which he feels are watching him, continues to frighten him, and so he covers the painting with a sheet. But when he looks back at it, he sees that, not only is the sheet missing, but also that the man has leapt outside the frame. Remarkably the man unties a sack with 1,000 gold-rouble packets, clearly labeled, inside. The old man begins to unwrap and rewrap the packets and then places them back in his sack. One of these packets falls to the side, and Chartkov snaps it up, clutching it fearfully to his chest. He awakens in a cold sweat, wondering whether it was a dream. He watches the man return to the frame and feels the residual weight of something that he had been holding in his hand and is unsure.

The next day, Chartkov is able to pay his rent with the money from the gold-rouble packet that is discovered fortuitously in the frame of the painting. He rejoices in his good luck, calculating that he will be able to truly cultivate his talents as a painter without worries of survival. This noble thought is fleeting, for he is seized by the desire for material goods. He goes to a tailor for new clothes, buys perfume, rents a lavish apartment, goes to the hairdresser, dines in fancy restaurants, and in general, indulges himself. He is so beset with an intense desire for fame that he pays for an article to be written about his talents in the newspaper.

Sure enough, the hyperbolic article brings clients, for the very next day, an aristocratic woman and her daughter Lise arrive at Chartkov's apartment. The woman hires him to paint her daughter's portrait, which he begins to do immediately. What she really wants is a replication of a portrait of Lise once done by a Monsieur Nohl, a name which means "zero" in Russian, obviously a comment on the lack of artistic identity and skill of the man. This mention has the important effect of foreshadowing how Chartkov, in painting such a portrait, will lose his own capability to create great art. From then on, he cannot concentrate on any other work; he is in a constant state of anticipation for the return of the woman and her daughter for another sitting, all the while distracting himself with more luxuries.

The woman and Lise return, and while painting the latter's

likeness, he becomes completely absorbed in his work, in a way that he has not since the arrival of the evil portrait. Chartkov paints a realistic, but not vanity-serving, portrait, and the woman forces him to change it to make her daughter more attractive. Later, he takes up a sketch of Psyche that he had begun earlier and inadvertently fills it with the features of the girl. The aristocratic woman is thrilled with the results, under the wrong impression that this is Lise's portrait. Immediately she wants her own portrait painted "in the guise of Psyche." Chartkov wants to touch up the Psyche painting, feeling guilty that it is not a true-to-life portrayal of the girl, but the woman is adamant about keeping it the way it is. Chartkov realizes that people want him to take liberties with their appearance, and that by not being too literal in his representation, he can obtain more clients. Indeed, he is flooded with commissions, all by people who allot no time for an artist's vision to deepen and all with specific demands regarding the nature of how they will be represented. He gives his talent over completely to the superficial art expected of a society painter.

Chartkov begins to fully live the life of a fashionable painter: he dines out, goes to balls and gallery openings, and fully gives himself over to the elite public. His indulgent life, attitudes about painting, and devotion to fame mark him as radically changed from the modest painter with high artistic ambitions that he once was. He gradually becomes tired of the same people, poses, and attitudes; he paints without any enthusiasm. He often begins a painting and has his assistants finish it for him. His forms are monotonous and so his brushstrokes become so as well; his imaginative powers cease and his creativity disappears. All that matters to Chartkov now is money. Gold becomes his passion, his ideal, his joy, his motivation, and also his fear. It is this fear of losing the gold he has amassed that makes him become a miser, a hoarder.

One day, Chartkov, due to his respected status as an elder statesman of painting, is invited to the Academy of Art to judge a new work sent from Italy by a Russian artist who is studying there. The man, a former friend of his, had devoted his life tirelessly to the pure study of art, eschewing all worldly goods and the opinions of others. Chartkov is met with a work of unspeakable beauty and is awestruck by its perfection. In this one work everything seems to coalesce: the study of Raphael's poses, the study of Correggio's brushwork, but most importantly, the power of creation contained in the soul of the artist himself. What is most impressive about the painting is the manner in which the artist had absorbed the images of the external world, while simultaneously transforming them with his own creative impulses into something new, yet in harmony with nature. Gogol emphasizes that the work is a creation and not a mere copy of nature, again emphasizing the importance of striking a balance between exact replication and too great an inventiveness. Chartkov is so struck that he cannot express what he thinks of the work; he runs out of the hall, overcome with sobs.

This incident awakens his whole artistic being and his youthful ambitions; a metaphoric blindfold has fallen from his eyes. He realizes that he has sacrificed his talent for worldly success. But alas, his talent is gone; he cannot paint creatively like he used to. It is as if his years of rote painting have rendered him incapable of anything but formulaic schemes. He recognizes that the portrait, which gave him his monetary beginning, has been the cause of his artistic corruption, and he orders it out of the house. Chartkov is seized by a terrible envy, which is mixed with rage. These hateful feelings are especially stirred in him whenever he sees a work of some talent, compelling him to buy up all great works of art to destroy. And so, just as money helps obscure his talent by motivating the creation of superficial art, it also aids in destroying the profound, the masterpieces.

Attacks of rage and madness visit Chartkov more frequently, and finally they turn into an illness. He begins to imagine the eyes of the portrait, and he hallucinates that the people around his bed are horrible portraits. Portraits seem to hang around him, all with animated eyes fixed on him. The doctor he enlists tries to make a connection between the visions he imagines and his illness, but cannot. Finally, after much agony, Chartkov dies, leaving behind no fortune, save the slashed masterpieces.

Part II of "The Portrait" begins in a completely different vein. We are placed in the middle of an auction where various antiques and wares are being sold. The portrait of the old man in the Asiatic costume receives much attention, and a bidding war arises. People are most struck by the liveliness of the eyes. When there are only two bidders remaining, an onlooker, "painter B.," begins to speak authoritatively. He states that if the people present listen to his story, he will prove that he has a right to the painting.

Painter B. describes a poor section of the city called Kolomna whose inhabitants are often forced to use the services of moneylenders. He tells of one particular moneylender, who, with his Asiatic garb and other distinguishing features, fits the description of the man in the portrait. This man differed from all the other moneylenders in that he was able to loan any sum of money to anyone. What is unusual, though, is that those who borrowed from him all ended their lives in some unfortunate way. Painter B. goes on to recount two such examples in great detail, after which he mentions innumerable others that fell victim to the moneylender. He then goes on to say that his father is the real subject of the story.

The father, a man of great strength of character, was an artist of great skill, who turned to Christian subjects in his work in his later years. For one particular commission for the Church, he had to include the devil; he immediately thought of the moneylender's visage as the perfect model. Then, fortuitously, it seemed to him, the moneylender appeared at his door, asking him to paint his portrait.

The father began to paint the portrait, all the while growing more excited with every feature he captured. But with each feature, especially the eyes, he felt more and more distressed and fearful. For this reason, he told the moneylender that he could not complete the portrait. The moneylender was very distraught; he was convinced that the portrait would ensure that he would not die entirely, and he asserted that must be present in the world. The morning of the next day, the father received the unfinished portrait from the moneylender; that evening, he heard that the moneylender had died.

After this death, the father was gripped with anxiety and began to act strangely. The painter's attempt to reproduce reality with absolute precision brought about the supernatural in the portrait. Its evil began to infiltrate his life and everyone else's with whom it would later come in contact. Uncharacteristically, he was envious of the success of one of his pupils, and to compete with him, he entered a contest to paint the paintings in a newly constructed church. The father's entry was first thought to be miraculous and a sure winner, but then it was observed that there was no holiness in the faces and something demonic in the eyes. Indeed, the father had painted the eyes of the moneylender into almost all of the faces. And so his picture was rejected, and his pupil won first prize. The father went into a rage, and he tried to burn the portrait of the moneylender. He was stopped by a fellow artist friend who asked him for the painting. The friend took the portrait away, and it was as if an enormous burden was lifted from the father's soul. He immediately regretted his wicked feelings and change in character, and believed that his portrait lost the prize because God was punishing him for the motivations behind it.

The friend who took the portrait was equally tormented by it, and gave it to his nephew, who sold it to an art collector, who sold it to someone else. When the father heard of this chain of events, set off by a portrait that he had been responsible for creating, he was convinced that his brush had served as the instrument of the devil. He suffered three deaths: those of his wife, daughter, and son, and believed it was heaven's punishment.

Painter B. relates how his father enrolled him in the Academy of Art at age nine and then withdrew to a monastery. When the superior of the monastery heard that the father had been a painter, he asked him to paint the central icon in the church, but the father refused, claiming that he would have to purify himself first. He began to live a more and more ascetic life, but even this penitence was not enough for him, and so he retreated to the wilderness. After strengthening his body and his soul through prayer, he returned to the monastery, and said that he was ready to paint. He went on to paint a transcendent rendition of the Nativity of Jesus, which compelled people to say that his brush had been guided by a holy power and that it had been blessed by heaven. He succeeded in creating a painting that fulfills the principles that should govern the artist as well as the work of art.

When painter B., at age twenty, had finished his studies, he went to visit his father before going off to Italy. His father gave him invaluable advice, learned through much hardship. He told him, among other things, not to ruin his talent, the most precious of God's gifts. He emphasized the importance of looking inward when representing the external world. While he was painting the moneylender, he had stifled his inner feelings in a slavish desire to be faithful to nature. This point is another echo of the theme on the ideal way to represent the external world that runs throughout "The Portrait." Painter B.'s father told him that art contains a hint of the divine and this makes it higher than any other thing in the world. He heightened the responsibility of the artist by asserting that he who has talent must be purer in soul than all others. The father finished his lesson by making painter B. promise that were he ever to come across the evil portrait, he would destroy it.

And so fifteen years later, painter B. appeals to the crowd to allow him to fulfill this promise. He looks toward the portrait on the wall, and the crowd does the same, but the painting is not there. Someone has taken it while the painter has been recounting the tale. The reader is left with many lingering questions: is painter B.'s story even true or just an elaborate ruse to distract the audience so that an accomplice could make off with the portrait? If it the story itself is true, is painter B. even connected to it? Did someone unrelated to painter B. and his story steal it? Or due to its supernatural tendencies, did the painting merely vanish of its own accord? We are also never told at what point in the chronology the Chartkov section occurs, before or after this auction scene, which heightens the enigma. All we are left with is a sense of mystery, as inexplicable as the fantastical story itself.

# "The Portrait"

**Chartkov** is the main character in the first section of "The Portrait." He is a struggling artist with a promising talent, but in whom his professor sees a propensity for becoming a fashionable painter as well as having a weakness for material goods. The portrait he buys, which provides him with money, only seals his doom.

**The Aristocratic Woman** asks Chartkov to paint a portrait of her daughter **Lise**, having seen the article that Chartkov printed about himself. She represents the philistine mentality of elite society that forces artists like Chartkov to forsake their talent.

**The Moneylender** is the subject of the portrait. In life, he was an evil man whose clients all ended their lives in ruin after borrowing money from him. In death, his destructive influence lives on, for anyone who comes into contract with his portrait also suffers a terrible fate. He can be said to be an incarnation of the devil.

**The Father-Painter** is the artist of the portrait of the moneylender. Upon painting the portrait, he is transformed into an angry and jealous man and so refuses to complete the evil work. It is too late, however, as the painting has begun to destroy all those who cross its path. For this reason, he withdraws to a monastery to purify himself, and is eventually redeemed through his art.

**Painter B.** is the narrator of the second section of "The Portrait." He is the son of the painter of the portrait and is an artist himself. He stakes his claim to the portrait to fulfill a promise that he makes to his father to destroy the evil portrait if given the opportunity.

# "The Portrait"

## LEONARD J. KENT ON AMBIVALENCE AND UNREALITY

[Leonard J. Kent is the author of *The Subconscious in Gogol' and Dostoevskij, and its Antecedents* from which these excerpts are taken. In his discussion of "The Portrait," Kent points to Gogol's ambivalent treatment of the artist Chartkov. He also shows how the dream about the portrait and the gold coins has the effect of suffusing the rest of "The Portrait," the conscious moments, with an air of unreality.]

Gogol's attitude toward Čartkov is somewhat ambivalent, much to the benefit of the story. Being a destitute artist, he is at first positively depicted, but his comprehension of art is imperfect because his inspiration is imperfect. He has talent, "but no patience". Gogol's attitude seems to be verbalized by the warning of the professor: "Take care. The outside world begins to attract you.... forget about fineries ... your own time will not fail to come". There is something of the materialist in Čartkov. As the narrator calmly informs us, "the professor was partially correct". But Čartkov's imperfect inspiration, his desire for money and what it can buy, are partially born of his very deprivation. Also, he is alienated, totally without friends or family, and his outcry, "Damn it! What a miserable world!", is therefore comprehensible. An artist who is something of a fop, talented but impatient, estranged, of "sensitive imagination and nerves", and destitute, Čartkov has about him the complexity of humanity, and it is clear that he is a double, in Gogol's terms. He contains the seeds of morality, the potential for immorality. (...)

The anticipatory function of the dream is fulfilled when Čartkov discovers the coins. At this point, because the gold pieces are precisely in the amount and in the shape he had dreamed, he once more asks "Isn't this all a dream?" The original dream, therefore, whether merely a dream or whether a manifestation of delirium brought on by subconscious guilt, continues to directly influence the story. It cloaks what follows in an aura of unreality. As the predictions implicit in the dream come true they reflect back on the dream, endowing it with supernatural prescience, and coloring the story with an aura not so much Gothic as mystical.

—Leonard J. Kent, *The Subconscious in Gogol' and Dostoevskij, and its Antecedents*. The Hague: Mouton & Co., 1969: 82, 83–84

## DONALD FANGER ON THE ARTIST'S FATE

[Donald Fanger is the Slavic Faculty Associate at the Davis Center for Russian and Eurasian Studies at Harvard University. He is the author of *Dostoevsky and Romantic Realism (Studies in Russian Literature and Theory)*. In this excerpt, he explores the artist's fate.]

"The Portrait" extends the theme of the artist's fate in Petersburg, making literal the presence of the devil and sharpening the question of the moral ambiguity of esthetic values. In part a disquisition on esthetics, in part an exploration of romantic demonology, it draws on motifs, ideas, and structures to be found in Wackenroder, Hoffmann, Maturin (whose *Melmoth the Wanderer* appeared in Russian in 1833), and Balzac— and shows analogies with a number of other works—popular at the time.[35] As usual, Gogol's debts are difficult to pinpoint as such, but the loss is not great. What is most important is the fact that he is accepting a series of already fading conventions here, rather than turning them to fresh use. In "The Portrait" he forgoes the comic along with narrative polyphony in the interests of a high seriousness which he would only later recognize might be available without such crippling sacrifice. The result is an allegorical fable, rendered in terms of apocalyptic earnestness— a mixture that Russian critics have insisted on calling tragic.

Subsequently revised and considerably expanded, the story as it appeared in *Arabesques* tells of a poor young painter, Chertkov, who is mysteriously drawn to a portrait with uncanny living eyes, buys it, finds money in the frame and customers for his own work suddenly at his door. Under the baneful influence of his acquisition, he becomes facile and fashionable, dooms his own talent, turns maniacally jealous of real creations (which he buys up only to destroy), and ends in madness, quickly followed by death. All this comprises only the first half of the story; the second (like the ending of "A Terrible Vengeance") provides the *Vorgeschichte* that explains his fate by telling how a Petersburg moneylender, possessed by the Antichrist, had persuaded a painter to prolong his evil existence by incarnating it on canvas. The painter, later repentant, redeems his compliance by becoming a hermit and icon painter; and his son—who tells the story at an auction where the portrait is for sale—completes the redemption, as his father has charged him to do, by telling the story during the first full moon exactly fifty years after the portrait was made. The portrait metamorphoses into an innocuous landscape, and the story ends.

Demonism and moralizing aside, Gogol's passionate estheticism produces a cloudy message about the "horrible reality" art can reveal when it pursues nature too slavishly.[36] The suggestion seems to be that God and the Devil are copresent in the world and that any representation of phenomena must serve one side or the other. The artist who succumbs to vanity and courts social acceptance—or even the artist who allows himself to pursue the phantom of truth unguided by a vision of beauty-does the Devil's work. Here is adumbrated a defense of Gogol's own concern with the banal and the trivial. For the artist, nothing in nature has fixed value; everything depends upon the quality and intention of the imagination behind each concrete rendering. But there is another inference to be drawn from "The Portrait": the world as such needs to be redeemed by art. Redemption lies in the conferring of value and meaning on what is otherwise a void, a "horrible reality"—ordinary human experience, which is for Gogol increasingly the realm of dead souls.

NOTES

35. The editorial notes to the Academy edition of Gogol's works cite analogues and probable sources in Wackenroder, Hoffmann, Maturin, and Balzac (III, 671–672); Gippius adds the names of Washington Irving, Spinello, and Pushkin as author of "The Queen of Spades"(*Gogol*, pp. 55–56). But of course

the theme of demonic intervention, like the themes of art and the artist, was in full vogue when Gogol wrote his story. In 1833 Nadezhdin had declared in *The Telescope* that for art "the material fidelity of a representation alone is not sufficient; it should breathe the life of reality and illumine the gloomy chaos of events with a single [guiding] idea. And only so it can find justification for its sovereign freedom in dealing with reality, reordering and changing events so that they may more clearly and fully express a predetermined idea." The realism dominant in France, Nadezhdin found, was "of a particular kind, an extremely dangerous realism"; were it to prevail entirely, "it would be impossible to believe either in God or in the dignity of the soul, for the world which this poetry develops before our eyes is a world without Providence or freedom." *Teleskop*, nos. 3 and 4, 1833; quoted in Kozmin, N.K. Nadezdin, pp. 389-390.

36. Here is the central passage in all its cumbersome opacity:

> " 'What is this?' he thought to himself: 'art, or some supernatural sorcery which has eluded the laws of nature? What a strange, what an incomprehensible thing to do! Or is there for man some boundary to which higher cognition leads and which, once he has crossed it, he is already stealing something uncreatable by the labor of man, tearing something alive out of the life that animates the original. Why is it that this crossing of the boundary set as a limit for the imagination is so horrible? Or is it that beyond imagination, beyond creative afflatus, reality at length follows—that horrible reality, into which imagination springs from its axis in consequence of some accidental push, that horrible reality which appears to him who thirsts for it when, desiring to comprehend the beauty of man, he arms himself with an anatomist's scapel, lays bare the interior and beholds the repulsiveness of man. Incomprehensible! Such an astonishing, horrible animation! Or is excessively close imitation of nature just as cloying as a dish that has an excessively sweet taste?'" (Ill, 405–406)

This first version of the story (from *Arabesques*) seems to condemn realism from the point of view of romantic aspiration; the revised version of 1842 seems rather to condemn mere copying in favor of a "higher" realism. Gogol claimed to have "entirely reworked" the story in Rome (XII, 45); for an unusually interesting discussion of the sense of this reworking, see A.L. Volynskij [A. L. Flekser], *Bor'ba za idealizm* (St. Petersburg, 1900), pp. 259–267.

—Donald Fanger, *The Creation of Nikolai Gogol.* Cambridge: Harvard University Press, 1979: 113–115.

## ROBERT LOUIS JACKSON ON REALITY

[Robert Louis Jackson is the BE Bensinger Professor Emeritus of Slavic Languages and Literatures at Yale

University. He is a scholar of nineteenth-century Russian literature, specializing in the works of Dostoevsky, Turgenev, and Chekhov. His own publications include *Dostoevsky's Quest for Form* and *The Art of Dostoevsky*. In his comments on the story, Jackson believes that the artist's attempts to imitate reality too closely actually leads to the supernatural, the unreal. Jackson makes a connection between the story's supernatural element and Gogol's own state of mind. He also states the tripartite reason behind the psychic illness that drives the story.]

On the fantastic plane of the story's action the effort to imitate reality results in the reification of the evil spirit of the moneylender. The devil breaks through the defenses of everyday reality. In purely aesthetic terms the painter's attempt to reproduce reality with absolute exactitude leads to the "super" natural, to a kind of magic realism, to a picture of reality, finally, that not only pushes realism to its limits and beyond but evokes in the viewer a disturbing sense of the uncanny, the unnatural, the grotesque. The viewer, full of apprehension and anxiety, finds himself on the threshold of the supernatural or fantastic. Instead of elevating his spirit, the portrait plunges him into serious distress or depression. He experiences a psychological crisis. ( ... )

To conclude: Gogol in "The Portrait" seems to be reflecting upon his own art, his own strange, disturbed, "super" natural intuitions of reality and upon the state of mind, aesthetic and psychological, that summons up his monsters from the deep. As we have seen, psychic illness in the story is attributed in part to the evil influence of the portrait, that is, to the supernatural; socially, it is attributed to the evil of gold; aesthetically, to a false conception of the relation of art and reality. The door is at least open, I suggest, to a conception of psychic disorder itself as responsible for the vision of evil.

—Robert Louis Jackson, "Gogol's 'The Portrait': The Simultaneity of Madness, Naturalism, and the Supernatural." *Essays on Gogol: Logos and the Russian Word*, eds. Susanne Fusso and Priscilla Meyer. Evanston: Northwestern University Press, 1992: 106, 111.

# DEREK MAUS ON THE DEMONIC ELEMENT

[Derek Maus is Assistant Professor of English at SUNY-Potsdam. He is the author of *A Companion to Fyodor Dostoevsky's* Crime and Punishment. *In this excerpt, he explores the demonic in "The Portrait."]*

The writing Gogol produced in the later stages of his career demonstrates a considerable affinity for this sort of metaphorical internalization of the devil and of devilish forces. A technique using verbal associations or allusions rather than direct depictions to bring a demonic element into his writing displays a significant refinement of the somewhat derivative stories of folk-devils and witches that he wrote earlier in his career. A quick comparison of the two versions of his story "The Portrait" illustrates how Gogol's narrative mode evolved from one in which the devil is clearly named and identified to one in which he is merely alluded to. The revision of the name of the main character of the first portion of the tale is a telling example of this transformation. The "Chertkov" of the 1835 version is a significantly more suggestive linkage to "chert," (the Russian word for "devil") than the "Chartkov" of the 1842 revision.(FN10) Also the character of the evil moneylender from the second portion of the story changes from one who is defined as "possessed of the devil" and whose "money possessed the power of being incandescent and burning through things, and ... marked with strange symbols" ("The Portrait" [vers. 1] 146) to one described as causing "a strange fate [in] all those who had borrowed money from him: all came to a miserable end" ("The Portrait" [vers. 2] 2: 290).(FN11) While his character in the second version is still associated with evil and even with demons and devils (the painter describes him as "the model of the devil" [2: 295] for his portrait of The Prince of Darkness), he is no longer directly and explicitly described as being in the service of the devil (and bearing physical signs thereof, in the form of the money).

Sylvie Richards maintains that Gogol's aim in creating this story (she, somewhat problematically, works only with the first version) is the same as is Hawthorne's in his similarly-themed sketch "The Prophetic Pictures": "the artist becomes at once diabolical creator and also self-creation within the framework of his art, seemingly shifting from two dimensions to three dimensions" (311). This idea corresponds with Hawthorne's already-cited ideas about the moral ambiguity of artistic creation, and Gogol's use of it in the 1835 version of "The Portrait" corresponds not only with his own unfixed ideas about the moral role of the author-artist but also with the standard romantic topos of incarnating evil through the act of artistic creation. The direct influence of Hoffmann, Tieck, Sir Walter Scott, Washington Irving, and other writers of Gothic romances has been catalogued extensively by Gogol scholars, but Gogol eventually outgrew the artistic possibilities for expression that the heavily-coded formula of the romantic/fantastic mode (FN12) afforded him. This artistic development pushed him in the direction of works like The Inspector General or Dead Souls, in which the relationship between good and evil is considerably more complicated and ambiguous than in most of the stories of Evenings on a Farm Near Dikan'ka or Mirgorod. Even the so-called "Petersburg" tales show a considerable degree of distancing from the standard conventions employed by the German Romantics and their descendants.

> —Derek Maus, "The Devils in the Details: The Role of Evil in the Short Fiction of Nikolai Vasilievich Gogol and Nathaniel Hawthorne." *Papers on Languages & Literature* 38, no. 1 (Winter, 2002): 91–92.

## NOTES

10. There is also some sound (albeit not morphological) correspondence with the words "cherta" (line of character trait) and, less closely, "chernovik" (rough draft). Given both the internalization of evil that Chertkov represents and the devi within the manuscript associated with him, it is not unreasonable to preceive him as a personification of a "chertovskaia cherta" (devilish trait) or "chertovskii chernovik" (devilish draft). Also, Robert Louis Jackson notes that in the 1835 version "the narrator makes it plain tht a 'line' ('cherta') or 'boundary' ('granitsa') separates the [physical world from both the spiritual and demonic realms.] The artist crosses it at his peril, that is, he crosses over the line (cherta) into the realm of the devil (chert)" (108). These potential associations are

tempered, if not largely lost, with the renaming that occurs in the second version of the story.

11. All quotations of Gogol's words are taken from The Complete Tales of Nikolai Gogol unless otherwise noted.

12. By this, I do not mean to imply that these formulas did not lead to some examples of first-rate writing. The sheer volume of romantic-derived work that arose in the early 1800s in response to the popularity of Hoffmann and other (and the repetition of stock plots, themes, characters that critics point out at every turn, even while lauding Gogol), however, leads to an inevitable exhaustion of this literary style, at least until the French Decadents revived it near the end of the century.

# "Nevsky Prospect"

"Nevsky Prospect" was first published in *Arabesques* (1835). The story is about expectation and deception, external appearances and internal truth, and the conflict between dream and reality. Divided into two sections, it tells the story of two contrasting men, an artist and a soldier, who are representative of the men of their respective professions.

The story is one of contrasts that are constantly illuminated throughout the tale. Piskarev is an artist who is serious, sensitive, and uncertain; Pirogov is a soldier who is flippant, coarse, and confident. Piskarev's quest of his woman is motivated by a desire for a chaste, idealistic, and deep love; Pirogov's quest is a lusty, superficial one. The nature of both their personalities and their quests make them react in dramatically different ways to the way their fates are played out. Piskarev obsesses about his inability to reconcile the ideal with reality and commits suicide, whereas Pirogov shrugs off his defeat and forgets about it.

"Nevsky Prospect" is also a story about art, and in this regard, the two men also diverge. They have different aesthetic ideals. For Piskarev, beauty of form and content must be identical, whereas for Pirogov, form alone is important and even has the power to improve content. In designing the story in this opposing manner, Gogol succeeds in creating an intricately symmetrical story that Pushkin called "the fullest" of Gogol's works. But despite the division of the story into two sections, Gogol succeeds in accomplishing a unity by enclosing the story within a frame: it begins and ends with a discussion of Nevsky Prospect, St. Petersburg's main street.

The story begins with the narrator's wondrous panegyric of Nevsky Prospect. The thoroughfare that gives the story its name is almost like a principal character in its own right. It is extolled for its many attributes, bringing immense pleasure to all: young, old, man, woman. It is the only place that people do not go to out of necessity; it is a place of sheer festivity. The street even makes those who frequent it seem to be better people. Nevsky Prospect is very important, for it serves as a communicatory link among the people who inhabit the various sections of St. Petersburg.

The narrator then moves on, in the same reverential tone of voice, to describe in meticulous, rich detail the various changes that the street undergoes from morning through night, in a manner which makes the street seem to come alive with a vibrant energy. He uses hyperbole to great effect in order to reinforce the notion of the street as an independent agent that wields power.

Nevsky Prospect can also be thought of as representing St. Petersburg as a whole, an example of the device of synecdoche (a type of metonymy where one part stands for the whole). And by extension, St. Petersburg can stand for cities and the world in general. Gogol also uses the device of synecdoche in describing the types of people on the street by their representative clothing and accessories. Against the backdrop of the constantly mutating street, man's search for woman and love is played out; the first episode is tragic while the second is farcical.

As the first episode begins, we witness a conversation between two people: Piskarev and Pirogov. Both men have glimpsed two women who catch their fancy, and their reactions to the situation reveal how different they are. Pirogov is confident in his decision to follow the blonde who strikes him, while Piskarev is timid and does not think of pursuing the brunette by whom he is captivated until Pirogov urges him.

Piskarev is an artist, a rare specimen in St. Petersburg, the reader is informed, and the characteristics of such a man are explained. In this way, the general personality traits of this profession are used to explain the behavior and reactions of one man. It is a kind of reverse synecdoche, with the whole standing for the part.

Piskarev chases after the brunette, her occasional fleeting looks bewitching him and filling him with desire. All of his senses are inflamed with passion, and everything in him trembles. To him, all things seem to be covered by mist, and he wonders whether it is all a dream. Piskarev follows her into a building, and because he thinks of her as a divinity, one who has descended from a "holy" place, the sordid surroundings both astonish and shock him. He wonders how such a beautiful creature could be associated with such a squalid environment, a house of prostitution. When she speaks, he has a similar reaction, thinking her words foolish and trite, and hardly befitting her captivating beauty. He is so distraught that he cannot listen to her any more, and he runs into the street.

The narrator, ostensibly giving voice to Piskarev's musings, then launches into an explanation on why the artist is so disturbed: the woman's beauty has been corrupted by depravity. And in a dramatic vein, he proclaims that she has been flung by an "infernal spirit," who wishes to destroy the harmony of life, into the "abyss." Piskarev is in love with the idea of the woman, but not the woman as she really is. He has reduced her to an object, something to be painted on a canvas.

That night, Piskarev has a dream in which he is visited by a stable boy who comes with an invitation from the woman and a carriage to take him to her. He is taken to a house and led to a richly decorated room that is filled with many people. Piskarev is overwhelmed by the multitude of different faces, the opulent fabrics, the diversity of languages; in short, his senses are overcome. He catches sight of the woman, who is one of the dancers performing there, but when he realizes that he is in his shabby painting clothes, he becomes ashamed and cannot face her. He presciently exclaims that her beauty will destroy him. When she finishes dancing, she asks him if he is bored, and says that she thinks he hates her. He does not have a chance to answer coherently, for the woman is swept away by another man. She does return, however, instructing him to meet her at the other end of the room. There, she tells him that she understands that he must have been confused by their first meeting, implying that she is not of the class of women with whom he saw her in the sordid apartment. She makes him promise that he will keep the secret of such a mystery once it is revealed to him. But she is immediately drawn away, and Piskarev loses her in the crowd. He awakens to find that it has all been a dream. He is rushed back to the gray disorder of his room at which point he utters a pivotal statement: "Oh, how repulsive reality is!"

Every day, Piskarev rushes through his life, looking forward to nighttime when he hopes to dream, to be transported back to the woman. He succeeds in dreaming, but only of useless things; he is not able to recapture his dream of the woman. In short, dreams become the focus of his life; their possibility is the only thing that excites him. Eventually, he becomes unable to sleep, which devastates him since this is the only instrument to dream. He begins to smoke opium as a means to restoring sleep, and by extension, his dreams of his desired woman.

The opium allows him to see the woman in dreams once again, but this ability makes his existence even worse, for he is disappointed and upset every time he wakes up. He thinks it would be better if she were not alive but an artistic creation, a kind of muse whom he could summon whenever he desires to paint the divine. And so he wishes that her real version, the woman of sordid surroundings, could be replaced by the inspired vision he has of her. Indeed, he is plagued by the conflict between fantasy and reality.

Through his dreams, Piskarev purifies the woman, completely transforming her in his mind. His favorite dream is one in which the woman acts as his virtuous wife. He gets the idea that the woman may have had some incident in her life which involuntarily drew her into degradation, and that maybe she actually wants to repent and draw herself out of her situation. He conceives of a plan in which she will atone for her sins, and then he will marry her, simultaneously returning this beautiful creature to the world. When he goes to enact his plan, she informs him that "they" brought her back drunk the last time she and Piskarev met. He wishes she were mute; nevertheless, he continues with his plan to reform her. She listens to him, while her friend looks on, but when he mentions that she will do handiwork by his side, while he paints, she asserts that she is no laundress or seamstress. He asks her to marry him, and her friend promptly makes fun of him.

This confrontation with the true nature of the woman is too much for Piskarev; it is impossible for him to transfer his dream of chaste and innocent love into the real world. He returns home and commits suicide with a razor. The horrible nature of his death is compounded by the fact that no one seems to care; he does not even warrant a funeral.

Piskarev tries to fix the rift between dream and reality by trying to change actuality; he does not succeed, and this is why he must leave the world. He learns that the harmony of life, which he imagines in his dreams, does not really exist. Appearances are not what they seem, and people and situations often cannot be placed in neat categories. Piskarev commits suicide because he sees the situation as irresolvable: life will always be a battle between dream and reality.

"Nevsky Prospect" then takes a different turn entirely, from the tragic and heavy to the comic and light. The narrator's tone changes from sympathetic to mocking as he shifts from Piskarev's failure to Lieutenant Pirogov's lascivious quest. Just as he did with Piskarev, the narrator takes a moment to situate the character of Pirogov by elucidating the general personality traits of those of his profession and their place in society. Again, it is an example of reverse synecdoche, with the whole standing for the part. Gogol takes advantage of the opportunity, in his description of Pirogov and those of his type, to mock the Russian bureaucracy and the importance placed on rank. It is also Gogol's chance to disparage Germans and their foreignness, as contrasted with native Russians in St. Petersburg.

Pirogov follows the blonde, who rebuffs his advances the whole time, to her home. There he encounters her husband Schiller, a cobbler, and his friend Hoffmann. Their conversation is in German, which Pirogov cannot understand, adding to the comic tone of this section; however, it is translated for the reader. Schiller, drunk, is expounding on his wish for Hoffmann, also drunk, to cut off his nose due to his habit—and its expense—of buying snuff. Before he can lose his nose, however, he notices Pirogov and is annoyed, ordering him to leave. Pirogov cannot believe that Schiller has ignored his officer rank, yet leaves, imputing the disrespect to drunkenness. The ridiculous slapstick quality of the scene contrasts sharply with the seriousness of the scenes in the Piskarev section. Even the names of the two Germans are crudely humorous, for the unrefined men share them with distinguished German authors.

Pirogov returns the next day, and the blonde continues to shun him, calling her husband to come out. Schiller is embarrassed to see someone who has seen him drunk and so tries to get rid of the lieutenant by quoting an inflated price to craft him a set of spurs. Pirogov agrees to the price, and Schiller, an "honest" German, feels a bit ashamed.

Despite the blonde's continued rejection of him, Pirogov refuses to give up his pursuit. He cannot fathom that someone could reject someone of his rank. We are told that the blonde is beautiful but stupid, after which the narrator then launches into a discussion of beauty and stupidity. Among other declarations, the statement is made that all inner flaws in a beauty become attractive, which is precisely the opposite of Piskarev's opinion.

The blonde proves exceedingly difficult to persuade, an obstacle which makes the prospect even more enticing in Pirogov's eyes. He returns often, ostensibly to ask about the spurs, but really to see her, and when these are finished, he asks Schiller to make him a sheath, to prolong his courtship further. Schiller, agrees to do the work, but becomes vexed when he sees Pirogov brazenly kiss his wife.

The narrator deviates to describe the character of Schiller, a diligent, frugal, and very exacting German, whose only vice is to drink once a week. Despite his controlled personality, Pirogov's behavior does make him jealous, but he cannot think of a way to get rid of him.

Having stupidly revealed that her husband is absent on Sundays, Pirogov pays her a visit one Sunday. He tries to get her to dance, since, in his mind, all German women stereotypically like to dance. When he kisses her, she begins to scream, and at that moment, her husband, Hoffmann, and another artisan return. Though we are not told how exactly they punish him, it is clear that Pirogov suffers injuries to his body, but more importantly to his pride. He plans on reporting the Germans to the police or to the state council or even to the sovereign himself.

But strangely enough, he does nothing of the sort. Having visited a pastry shop and read something from the newspaper, he already feels less angry. Due to the pleasant weather, he takes a stroll down Nevsky Prospect and feels still better. And then he attends a party, so enjoying himself that the event no longer bothers him.

There Pirogov's story ends, and the narrator's musings begin as he attempts to connect the two divergent paths that Piskarev and Pirogov take and their disparate fates. He ponders the nature of desire, whether one ever gets what he wants, and the arbitrary nature of fate and how it toys with humans. In his opinion, most strange of all are the events that occur on Nevsky Prospect. He warns us not to trust it or those who frequent it, for appearances on this street are deceptive. Most deceiving of all are the women. The idealistic Piskarev wants a woman in tune with his artistic ambitions, while the common Lieutenant Pirogov only has flirtation and an affair in mind. But on Nevsky Prospect nothing is what it seems. The poetic brunette turns out to be a prostitute, while the coy blonde ends up being a German housewife of unassailable virtue.

Everything having to do with the street is mired in deception, especially at night, when the devil himself lights the lamps to mask the truth. The narrator's revelation of this negative aspect of Nevsky Prospect stands in sharp contrast to his fervent adulation of the same street at the story's outset. It is as if the reader, like Piskarev and Pirogov, has been fooled by the seductions of an external appearance, which is not what it seems.

# LIST OF CHARACTERS IN
# "Nevsky Prospect"

**Piskarev** is one of the main characters of "Nevsky Prospect." He is an idealistic artist, who pursues a brunette whom he sees while walking on Nevsky Prospect. He is devastated when he discovers her sordid background, and turns to dreaming to satisfy his desire for her. Unable to reconcile these dreams with reality, he commits suicide.

**Pirogov** is the other main character of "Nevsky Prospect." He is a brash lieutenant who pursues a blonde for the purposes of a lusty dalliance. He is undeterred by her inviolable virtue, and is caught by her husband and his friends who beat him. Distracting himself with simple pleasures, he ends up forgetting about the whole incident. Gogol makes use of the character of Pirogov to deride the Russian bureaucracy and its emphasis on rank.

**The Brunette** is a prostitute whom Piskarev chases. Her exceptional beauty would seem to bespeak a corresponding inner loveliness, but this is not the case. She laughs at Piskarev's proposal of marriage, thereby leading to his suicide.

**The Blonde** is the German woman whom Pirogov chases. Her coy cuteness belies a strong virtuousness that the lieutenant is not able to violate.

**Schiller** is the German husband of the woman whom Pirogov pursues. He is very honest and proud of his work as a cobbler, qualities which allow Pirogov to extricate himself into the life of him and his wife. He is also frugal, orderly, and precise to an extreme degree, stereotypical German qualities. In fact, Gogol exploits the character of Schiller and his friends to mock Germans in general. The scenes involving him—and his friend Hoffmann—are very comical, in a ridiculous way.

# CRITICAL VIEWS ON
# "Nevsky Prospect"

## LEONARD J. KENT ON DOUBLING

[Here, Kent illustrates how the worlds and protagonists
of the two contrasting sections of "Nevsky Prospect," are
doubles of each other.]

The story is, then, part tragedy, part comedy. Devoid of the
fantastic, there is a brilliantly contrasted clash of different
worlds, that of the sensitive artist and that of Pirogov the
philistine. Dostoevskij understood the shallowness of Pirogov,
the necessity for Piskarevs.[34] Perhaps they are doubles, parts of
each in each. Piskarev, the dreams seem to suggest, could become
Pirogov; Pirogov must already be partly Piskarev. There is a
common denominator—flight. Both run from reality, both
dream to escape: Piskarev of what he cannot be, Pirogov of what
will make him forget what the world is. His cynicism is as
escapist oriented as Piskarev's romanticism. He is perhaps
Piskarev turned inside out.

## NOTE

34. Dostoevskij loathed philistines and philistinism. His rejection of *pošlost'* is
apparently not negative, as it is in Gogol's grotesques, but is a mystical vision of
salvation through suffering.

> —Leonard J. Kent, *The Subconscious in Gogol' and Dostoevskij, and
> its Antecedent:* The Hague: Mouton & Co., 1969: 76.

## JESSE ZELDIN ON THE INTERPLAY OF RELATIONSHIPS

[Jesse Zeldin is the author of *Nikolai Gogol's Quest for
Beauty: An Exploration of His Works* from which these

excerpts are taken. Here, Zeldin illuminates the complex relationships that exist between dreams, reality, truth, and the role of the artist in "Nevsky Prospect."]

A good third of Piskaryov's story takes place outside the realm of physical reality and in that of dreams. In these dreams the prostitute appears in complete and harmonious beauty, no longer the contradiction that she is in physical life. Obviously, this can all be viewed in psychological terms along the lines of wish-fulfillment and frustration, and such an approach is clearly valid within its own domain. I should like to suggest, however, that this approach is neither a necessary one nor the only valid one, especially if we subscribe to V. V. Zenkovsky's proposition that Gogol was a portrayer of types rather than of individuals. Viewed, therefore, in terms of the problem of reality, it may well be that Gogol was reversing the usual perception, that Piskaryov's dreams represent the truly real, while the prostitute's world is the falsely real. For it is in the former that beauty exists, in the latter that it does not; the former that tells the truth, the latter that deceives (we are reminded of the narrator's remark at the end that it is on Nevsky Prospekt that "everything is a dream"); the sight of the former that is especially vouchsafed the artist, the sight of the latter that is seized upon by most. The device of the dream is here used, in other words, less to make a psychological point about the workings of the human mind than it is to emphasize Gogol's idea of what constitutes truth. The story's pathos lies in Piskaryov's failure to realize that it is the artist's job to convey reality, not to invent it. This does not mean that the artist has no obligation to attempt to change human life. On the contrary, that is the very reason for his conveyance of reality, so that men may be brought to live in it. The difficulty is that most people either do not know, or they deliberately reject, the real; they choose, as "The Portrait" and "Nevsky Prospekt" show, what is false.

—Jesse Zeldin, *Nikolai Gogol's Quest for Beauty: An Exploration into His Works*. Lawrence, Kansas: The Regents Press of Kansas, 1978: 40.

# VASILY GIPPIUS ON FULLNESS

[Although he wrote in verse in his early years and translated a number of foreign poets, Vasily Gippius (1890–1942) was primarily a scholar and critic of Russian literature. He taught at Perm and later worked at the Institute of Russian Literature (Pushkin House) of the Academy of Sciences in St. Petersburg. He wrote extensively on nineteenth-century topics, but he was primarily interested in Gogol. According to Maguire, his book, *Gogol*, remains the single best monograph on the writer in any language. The essay excerpted here is taken from a two-volume collection of original source materials and scholarly essays published in 1936. Here Gippius imputes the "fullness" of "Nevsky Prospect" not only to the variety of character-types, but also to the combined elements of tragedy and farce.]

Pushkin had good reason to call "Nevsky Prospect" the fullest of Gogol's works.[20] Its "fullness" depends not only on the variety of character-types, but also on the combination of the two elements of Gogol's art: tragedy, which underlies the ideology and psychology of the story, and farce, which is the most finished and symmetrical element as far as the structure is concerned. The ironic remarks of the author, which give higher relief to the caricature-like kaleidoscope of the street and the farce in Schiller's house, cease when Piskaryov's tragedy is being depicted: here the exclamations and questions on the part of the narrator take on an unmistakably pathetic quality and do not sound like authorial interventions, but rather, like a commentary on Piskaryov's experiences.

NOTE

20. [Review of second edition of EVENINGS ON A FARM NEAR DIKANKA, SOVREMENNIK, No. 1, 1836.]

—V.V. Gippius, *Gogol*, ed. and trans. by Robert A. Maguire. Ann Arbor: Ardis, 1981: 50.

# RICHARD A. PEACE ON THEMES

[Richard A. Peace is an Emeritus Professor in the Russian Department at the University of Bristol in the UK. He has published numerous articles and essays on Gogol, Dostoevsky, Chekhov, and Russian literature and literary studies in general. His six books include *The Enigma of Gogol: An Examination of the Writings of N.V. Gogol and their place in the Russian Literary Tradition.* In his consideration of "Nevsky Prospect," Peace discusses Gogol's use of synecdoche for purposes of characterization.]

The use of synecdoche says much about Gogol's attitude to characterisation: people in the story are presented in a purely external way; they are assessed by their exteriors. The narrator's imagination sees objects instead of human beings. The effect is dehumanising, and yet, at the same time, these objects in themselves are a further stimulus to the narrator's flights of fancy. His imagination, however, does not strive to penetrate; it does not treat the façade as a key to unlock the inner personality of the wearer of these clothes, these swords, these whiskers etc.,[6] quite the reverse: the narrator's imagination uses such externals as a starting point to move outwards towards fantasy, towards a view of the world which becomes increasingly more grotesque. It is a process in which the imagination is the vehicle for flight, away from any human content, towards a bizarre and ever increasingly dehumanised world of fantasy. (...)

The second story concerning Lieutenant Pirogov is obviously to be taken as an ironic comment on the sad tale of Piskarev. The narrator presents his second hero exactly as he had presented his first (and indeed as he does all the denizens of the Nevsky Prospekt) not so much as a character in his own right, but as a type. If Piskarev is the typical St Petersburg artist, then Pirogov is the typical St Petersburg lieutenant; both are introduced in the feigned 'sociological' manner which we see elsewhere in the story: 'But before we say who Lieutenant Pirogov was, it would not be harmful to relate something about the society to which Pirogov belonged' (III, 34). The 'sociological' method is, of course, entirely deceptive; it is merely a device of characterisation which substitutes the whole for the part. It is a reversal of the synecdoche, though, strangely enough, the effect is precisely the same; for the partial truth of the general is substituted for the fuller truth of the particular; the broader *surface*—for the deeper *content*. (...)

As these two contrasting tales in themselves suggest, a central theme of 'Nevsky Prospekt' is incongruity. Piskarev in the first story complains of the 'eternal discord between dream and reality' (*vechnyy razdor mechty s sushchestvennost' yu*). Yet the narrator himself, musing on both these stories as he walks along the Nevsky Prospekt, draws a moral in terms of desires: 'Do we ever get what we want? Do we ever achieve that for which it might appear our powers had been destined as though on purpose? Everything happens *vice versa*' (III, 45).

The examples of unrequited desires, with which the narrator further seeks to illustrate his theme of *vice versa*, seem grotesque in the context: a passion for horses and an appetite for food. Nevertheless the first example is merely the thwarted passion for the beautiful, which we see in Piskarev, brought down to a mundane and comic level, with horses, rather than women, as the exemplars of beauty: 'Fate has given one man the most beautiful horses, and he rides on them with indifference, not noticing their beauty at all, whereas another whose heart burns with horsey passion walks on foot and has to be contented with clicking his tongue whenever a trotter is led past him' (III, 45). The narrator's second illustration has relevance in a similar grotesque way for Pirogov, that lover of puff pastry: 'One man has an excellent cook, but unfortunately such a small mouth, that he just cannot get into it more than two pieces of food. Another has a mouth the size of the War Office Arch, but unfortunately he has to make do with any old German meal of potatoes. How strangely our fates play with us' (III, 45). Pirogov had 'a mouth as big as the War Office Arch', in as much as he wanted to complain to the War Office (*Glavnyy shtab*), but in the end he accommodated himself to the rough German 'hospitality' that had been meted out to him.[9]

By choosing two such grotesque pendants for his stories of Piskarev and Pirogov, the narrator is illustrating the theme of 'incongruity' in terms of the incongruous itself. No less incongruous is the juxtaposition of the two main stories themselves; for although one must obviously be taken as a comment on the other, their essential relationship is just as oblique and grotesque as the commentary provided by the narrator's two 'pendants'. They are a reflection of that eternal tension in Gogol's art between 'tears' (Piskarev) and 'laughter' (Pirogov). The story about the artist is in essence a sentimental tale about the hidden tears the world does not see;[10] the story of the lieutenant is permeated with a laughter which chastises overweening mediocrity more soundly than a physical drubbing.

## NOTES

6. A claim Gogol would later make about his depiction of reality in youth. Cf. *Dead Souls*, chapter 6 (VI, 110–11).

9. Cf. Schiller's own diet: 'He would in no circumstances increase his expenditure, and if the price of potatoes rose too much above what was usual, he would not add a single copeck, he would only reduce their quantity, and although he would sometimes remain a bit hungry, he would, nevertheless, get used to it' (III, 42).

10. Cf. the theme of 'pity' (*zhalost'*) in Piskarev's attitude to the prostitute (III, 22).

> —Richard Peace, *The Enigma of Gogol: An Examination of the Writings of N.V. Gogol and Their Place in the Russian Literary Tradition.* New York: Cambridge University Press, 1981: 98, 102–3, 104–5.

## GAVRIEL SHAPIRO ON EXPECTATIONS

> [Gavriel Shapiro is an Associate Professor in the Department of Russian Literature at Cornell University where he served as Department Chair from 1995 to 1998. Dr. Shapiro has published two books and a numerous articles, and in 1995, his *Nikolai Gogol and the Baroque Cultural Heritage* was selected by *Choice*, the journal of the American Library Association, as an outstanding academic book for the year. He demonstrates how the

contrasting plotlines of "Nevsky Prospect" serve to strengthen the main idea of the story, that the world does not conform to expectations.]

In "Nevsky Prospekt," Gogol turned again to antithesis as a compositional device, but this time he used it as a polemical tool. He built the narration on a juxtaposition of two plot lines, that of the idealistic, sensitive Piskarev and that of the vulgar, complacent Pirogov. The dissimilarity between the characters, each in his own way failing in his enterprise, was designed to emphasize the main idea of the tale—that in this demonic world, in which appearances differ sharply from reality, "Everything goes contrary to what we expect" (3:45; Kent, 1:237). Gogol's tale drastically deviates from and polemicizes against a Romantic approach, exposing the dreaminess of Piskarev and self-satisfied vulgarity of Pirogov as two sides of pseudo-life and pseudo-culture.[49]

NOTE

49. Cf. Dilaktorskaia, *Fantasticheskoe*, 31–32, and Markovich, *Peterburgskie povesti*, 72–74.

—Gavriel Shapiro, *Nikolai Gogol and the Baroque Cultural Heritage*. University Park, PA: The Pennsylvania University Press, 1993: 202.

# "The Nose"

Gogol wrote "The Nose," composed between 1833 and 1836, especially for the *Moscow Observer*; however, it was returned to him because it was considered too "sordid." The story, in a revised form, was eventually published in 1836 in the third edition of Pushkin's *The Contemporary*, with a note by Pushkin commenting on Gogol's reluctance to publish the story and the fact that he found much in it that was original, bizarre, and very humorous. Gogol revised it yet again in 1842 when the story came out in his collected works.

"The Nose" is the story of a man who not only wakes up one morning to find his nose missing, which would be fantastic enough as it is, but also finds it walking about in the guise of a person. A striking feature of the story is that, although some characters do question the feasibility of a nose becoming separate from its owner and walking around like a person, most of the participants treat the situation as a rational occurrence—an unusual one, yet one situated in the realm of possibility.

"The Nose" can be thought of in a multitude of ways. It can be considered as a satire on the milieu of the bureaucracy and officialdom. It can also be regarded as a story about the anxiety of status. And it can even be thought of as a dream or mere fantasy. What is remarkable about "The Nose" is its unorthodox nature, for in this narrative, cause and effect are completely disconnected. In fact, the tale can be defined by its ambiguities, the loose ends that defy inclusion in one comprehensive symbolic system. "The Nose" is also replete with incongruities; it has been said that the only principle of consistency in the story is that of inconsistency. Even critics seem to be confounded by the story, and much has been written about its resistance to interpretation.

The story, recounted by an omniscient narrator, is divided into three sections. The first involves a barber, Ivan Yakovlevich, who may or may not have something to do with a missing nose. The second centers on a collegiate assessor named Kovalev, who awakens one morning to find his nose missing. The third section brings these two characters together and tries to explain such a miraculous occurrence.

## I.

The first section introduces us to the barber Ivan Yakovlevich, who is distressed to find a nose in the middle of his breakfast bread. He recognizes it as belonging to the collegiate assessor Kovalev whom he shaves every Wednesday and Sunday. He cannot remember what occurred and is puzzled by the whole predicament.

Provoked by his wife's threats of reporting him to the police, he leaves to dispose of the nose. He throws the offending appendage into the river. Ivan Yakovlevich does not escape untainted, for a suspicious policeman asks him what he is doing on the bridge, and proclaims the barber's answers to be lies. The first section ends with the narrator elliptically saying that nothing more is known about this incident.

## II.

The second section commences with Kovalev awakening without his nose. We are given background on Kovalev to better understand how the loss of a nose will affect him and also to begin Gogol's ridicule of officialdom that will continue unabated throughout the story. Gogol hints that Kovalev has not earned his collegiate assessor position by means of a diploma, the proper route. Instead, it was obtained in the Caucasus, presumably by some illicit or corrupt means. Kovalev is a vehicle for Gogol to both mock and condemn the Russian bureaucracy and the emphasis placed on rank. He insists on being called "major," the military equivalent of his title, to impute more nobility and power to his personage. He is a man who finds nothing wrong with the abuse of inferior officers in plays, but can never pardon an attack on staff officers. Kovalev is also obsessed with power's inextricable partner: money. He maintains that the only way he will get married is if it were to someone with significant capital.

He has come to St. Petersburg with high hopes of finding a post that he considers suitable to his rank: that of vice-governor or an executive in a prominent department. His inflated sense of rank and lofty career ambitions coupled with his physical vanity make the loss of his nose all the more humorous, ironic, and to him, devastating. The loss of the nose means much more than the loss of an organ; it is a loss of identity, of self. For Kovalev, his career is his sense of self-worth, and he cannot advance his career without a nose. It also has another function: a social and sexual one, for without his nose, Kovalev cannot call on the ladies with whom he is acquainted. Thus, he equates both the loss of the nose with the loss of career prospects and the inability to make an advantageous marriage. In addition, innumerable essays have been written on the nose as phallic symbol and the sexual puns that exist throughout the story.

Kovalev decides to see the police chief about the matter, and on the way there, he catches sight of his nose, in the guise of a gentleman in uniform, getting out of a carriage and entering a building. He watches the man/nose exit the building, noting that his extravagant uniform would ascribe to him the position of state councillor, a higher rank than Kovalev himself holds. Kovalev does not know what to make of the situation and wonders how it is even possible. He follows the carriage and his nose into a cathedral. Inside, he tries to reason with the nose, who not only says that he is not Kovalev's nose, but also that there can be no close relationship between them since they are of such different ranks. To someone so rank-obsessed as Kovalev, the latter point is probably more galling.

Despite the realistic accounting of events, of the nose existing in its own right, it is possible that its existence as a separate entity is a result of Kovalev's subconscious. The nose can be viewed as a manifestation of Kovalev's desires, for example, to possess a higher rank, more power, and a fearless, imperturbable character. The nose seems to represent all of his worldly ambitions.

The police chief is not in, and Kovalev becomes very worried about the nose slipping out of the city before it could be caught. He decides to go to the newspaper office to take out an advertisement to this effect, but the newspaper clerk refuses to run such a seemingly ridiculous advertisement. The clerk takes pity on Kovalev, having been shown his flat face where his nose had been, and offers him a pinch of snuff. Seeing that he cannot even partake of this simple pleasure without a nose, Kovalev becomes even more upset.

Kovalev then goes to see the police commissioner, who is of no help and who insults him by implying that he has not acted respectfully, and that this is a habit of majors in general. Again, Kovalev is more disturbed by the affront to his rank than by a refusal to get help for his problem. He can pardon anything disparaging said about him except for those referring to his rank or title.

Abruptly and with no tangible evidence, he decides that his missing nose must be the work of Podtochina, the staff officer's wife, who wished him to marry her daughter. He is convinced that this is her way of exacting revenge on him for declining the offer of her daughter, and believes that she hired a sorceress to put a spell on him. While he is making plans to expose her, a policeman comes to the door with the news that the nose has been intercepted before it could leave town. The policeman also tells him that a chief participant in the matter is none other than his barber. The policeman gives him back his nose and leaves, but not before taking a monetary reward, another criticism of the Russian bureaucratic system.

Kovalev's problem is not solved, however, for he cannot seem to affix the nose to his face. He summons a doctor who is unable to do so either, and even says that it will be worse if he tries to attach it. Kovalev tries to appeal to the doctor to reconsider by saying that he has many important acquaintances, despite his having tried this tactic at the newspaper office to no avail. Kovalev then tries to bribe the doctor, but he refuses to treat him, stating that he does not treat people for profit.

Kovalev writes a letter to Podtochina in which he informs her that she will not compel him to marry her daughter in this manner, and that he will seek legal action if the nose is not returned. She writes back that she knows nothing about a nose, save if he meant the colloquial expression, to lead someone on, and in this case, she was not leading him on, but would give her daughter to him gladly. Kovalev promptly changes his mind, believing that the letter attests to the woman's innocence.

The Kovalev recounting abruptly stops, and the narrator tells of the public's recent fascination with the fantastic and the bizarre: magnetism, dancing chairs, etc. There are even alleged sightings of Kovalev's nose walking down the street. And just as at the end of the first section, the narrator declares that "the whole incident is shrouded in mist," and what happens later is unknown.

## III.

Gogol begins the third section with a statement that can be said to apply to the whole story and its outrageous premise: "Perfect nonsense goes on in the world." More directly, it refers to the inexplicable reappearance of Kovalev's nose on his face. One morning he wakes up, and it is there as if nothing had happened. Immediately after, Ivan Yakovlevich comes to give him a shave. The barber marvels at the nose, which he threw in the river and which has miraculously returned.

Kovalev's immediate and future happiness is recounted: he goes to a pastry shop, meets Podtochina and her daughter on the street, fills his nose with snuff, visits important people. In short, he lives his life in a constant state of euphoria. The account of this tale stops, and the narrator turns to more abstract musings.

He wonders at the improbability of the story and the supernatural nature of it. He then switches to a question which he says is most inconceivable, that is, the reason why authors pick such unworthy subjects to begin with. He ends by returning to the plausibility issue, reflecting that such strange incidents do not occur often, but do in fact occur in the world. We are left with the impression that perhaps we are not meant to understand everything in the world or in literature for that matter. The mist that Gogol uses to shroud the details of the story reinforces this impression. The incongruities in the story can be justified by reference to the absurdities of the real world. One interpretation is that the Kovalev story is merely one of the rumors that have been circulating around St. Petersburg, or it could be a bit of invented gossip, tossed about at a social gathering. Another possible way of looking at the story champions the importance of the imagination in filling in the holes that Gogol purposely leaves and connecting the loose ends that dangle between people and events. Or perhaps it is all a dream, for the word for "dream" in Russian is "*son*"—the word for "nose" in Russian backwards.

# "The Nose"

**Ivan Yakovlevich** is the barber who shaves the collegiate assessor Kovalev twice a week. He finds Kovalev's nose in his bread one morning, and does not know how it got there. Impelled by the threats of his wife Praskovya Osipovna, he disposes of the nose in the river.

**Major Kovalev**, the main character, is a collegiate assessor who has recently arrived in St. Petersburg to seek a position for himself, both in terms of a career and an advantageous marriage. He is obsessed by rank and its manifestations. This obsession with external appearances makes the disappearance of his nose all the more of a hardship for him.

**The Nose** is Kovalev's nose in the guise of a person. He is a state councillor, which is three ranks above Kovalev's own position, adding to Kovalev's distress. He is apprehended while trying to leave St. Petersburg and is returned to Kovalev.

**The Police Commissioner** is of no assistance to Kovalev in recovering his nose. In fact, he injures the man further by implying that he has acted impurely, as many of Kovalev's rank are wont to do.

**The Doctor** is not able to reattach Kovalev's nose, and much to Kovalev's chagrin, will not accept a monetary bribe to do so.

**Alexandra Podtochina** is a staff officer's wife whom Kovalev believes is responsible for the loss of his nose. He thinks that she hired a sorceress to cast a spell on him as revenge for his refusal to marry her daughter. In the end, he deems her innocent after reading a letter she sends him.

# "The Nose"

## IVAN YERMAKOV ON INTERNAL LOGIC AND THE DREAM

[Born in 1875, Ivan Yermakov was a practicing psychoanalyst, mentored by Freud, who had a strong interest in literature. He was the editor of a series, "The Psychological and Psychoanalytical Library," which published translations of works by such authorities as Freud, Jung, Reik, and MacDougall. His own books constituted the contributions to literary criticism in this same series: *Studies on the Psychology of the Art of A.S. Pushkin* and *Sketches for an Analysis of the Art of N.V. Gogol*. The latter contains an article, "'The Nose,'" from which the following excerpts are taken. In this passage, Yermakov discusses the notion of the internal logic of aspects of "The Nose" in the face of its seemingly nonsensical nature. He examines the role that the dream plays in revealing an individual's inner failings.]

For the present, however, we can draw two conclusions from our analysis of "The Nose." First of all, what strikes the reader as being mere chance, "nonsense," a dream yet not quite a dream; what makes Ivan Yakovlevich and Kovalyov constantly test themselves to see whether they are asleep or losing their minds— all this has its own logic and has been skilfully prepared by the author.[58] From here it is only a step to the assertion that sleeping and dreaming are not such nonsense after all. The statement that the nose was found by a near-sighted police officer with a mother-in-law who could not see anything either is fraught with significance. Does it not say that the real meaning of the loss of the nose can be discovered and revealed only when a person is near-sighted, when he can see nothing but his own nose, or, in other words, nothing but a dream? (...)

Gogol of course formulated his statements not in the dispassionate language of scientific propositions but in the language of imagery. The story makes it clear that Gogol grasped the significance of use the dream as a phenomenon that threatens us and compels us to give serious thought to ourselves. He discerned the possibility of crisis in Kovalyov's petty and intimidated soul—in his useless running around and in his cynical attitude toward women. He created a tragedy, a tragicomedy, and thereby posed the question: what is more important, the sexual or Kovalyov? Is the sexual subordinate to Kovalyov, or Kovalyov to the sexual? The nose comes off by itself and declares its independence of Kovalyov; so far as it is concerned, Kovalyov is nothing more than a carriage for it to ride in. Kovalyov laughs at himself for being foolish enough to take a dream for reality. He does not notice that it is precisely his predicament in the dream which perhaps does more than anything else to expose the emptiness of his life and the humiliation of being utterly dependent on his own nose. Whenever it seems as if the meaning of these events is about to be revealed, everything is shrouded in fog. Kovalyov is not allowed to see; he does not want to see the person who is to blame for everything: himself.[61]

NOTES

58. The chance happening is of interest, but it is legitimate in a work of art only when the writer puts it there *not by chance*. In a work of art, what may look like a chance happening on the surface is actually subject to the inner laws of the work.

61. Such dreams are by no means rare. I will mention, by way of example, the case of a twelve-year-old boy who dreamed that his nose had been cut off by a streetcar, and of a five-year-old boy who dreamed that he caught a scampering mouse, which he identified with his sex organ, after actually grasping his organ. For the symbolism of the organ, as a bird, a mouse, etc., see Part 2 of Freud's lectures.

—Ivan Yermakov, "The Nose.'" *Gogol from the Twentieth Century: Eleven Essays.*, ed. Robert J. Maguire. Princeton: Princeton University Press, 1974: 195, 197.

JESSE ZELDIN ON MATERIALISM

[Here Zeldin shows how the nose functions merely as one more valuable possession in the materialistic, status-driven world of "The Nose."]

No one asks—nor does Gogol indicate—how the nose grew to the stature of an official, then shrank back to a size proper to fit into a pocket. Such questions are quite beside the point of the actual possession of the nose; it is property. The nose is valuable because, like the title of Major, like a wife with a large dowry, or like the wearing of a medal (after the nose is restored to him, we are told, Kovalyov bought the ribbon of an order "for some unknown reason, since he was not a knight of any order himself"; 3:75), it lends a certain status to its owner, or, to be more accurate, its absence deprives him of a certain status, he believes. Other people have their possessions: the policeman his mother-in-law; the physician his "noble carriage"; the newspaper clerk his officiousness. And each defines himself in terms of his possessions.

—Jesse Zeldin, *Nikolai Gogol's Quest for Beauty: An Exploration into His Works*. Lawrence, KA: The Regents Press of Kansas, 1978: 52.


## ANN SHUKMAN ON INTERPRETATION

[Ann Shukman is a freelance writer and lecturer. Her publications include *Literature and Semiotics: A Study of the Writings of Yu. M. Lotman* and *The Semiotics of Russian Culture*, an annotated edition of essays by Yu. M. Lotman and B.A. Uspensky. Shukman, in attempting to elucidate "The Nose" in her essay "Gogol's 'The Nose' or the Devil in the Works," points to Todorov's opinion that "The Nose" actually resists any type of interpretation.]

(...) [T]he story took its place in Russian literature as a unique and dazzling example of the fantastic, that ambiguous genre where, to follow Todorov's definition:

the text obliges the reader to treat the world of the characters like a world of living people and to hesitate between a natural and a supernatural explanation of the events evoked ... refusing both an allegorical interpretation and a 'poetic' one.[23]

In the final (1842) version of the story Gogol pointed up this ambiguity in the last words of the closing paragraph: 'Whatever anyone may say such events do occur in the world—rarely, but they do occur' (*kto chto ni govori, a podobnyye proisshestiviya byvayut na svete,—redko, no byvayut* (III, 75)).

NOTE

23. Tzvetan Todorov, *Introduction à la littérature fantastique* (Paris, 1968) p. 37. (My translation, A.S.). Another way of treating the fantastic is to see the narrative as one in which more than one mutually exclusive *fabula* coexist in one *syuzhet*, see, Shlomith Rimmon-Kenan, 'Deconstructive Reflections on Deconstruction: In Reply to Hillis Miller' (*Poetics Today*, II, lb, Winter 1980/81, p. 185n.). In the case of *The Nose*, there are three *fabuly*: the barber's story, Kovalyov's loss of his nose and its restitution, and the story of the transformation of the nose into the state counsellor and back again.

> —Ann Shukman, "Gogol's 'The Nose' or the Devil in the Works." *Nicolay Gogol: Text and Context*. London: The Macmillan Press Ltd., 1989: 66–67.

## GARY SAUL MORSON ON CAUSATION AND ALLEGORY

[Gary Saul Morson is Frances Hooper Professor of the Arts and Humanities at Northwestern University. His publications include *The Boundaries of Genre: Dostoevsky's "Diary of a Writer" and the Tradition of Literary Utopia* and *Hidden in Plain View: Narrative and Creative Potentials in "War and Peace."* In "Gogol's Parables of Explanation: Nonsense and Prosaics" in which he discusses "The Nose," he dispels any causal linkages between events while also pointing to the myriad possible allegorical ones.]

Gogol has clearly made every effort to make causal linkage impossible to find. No one, at least, has found it, and we can be readily convinced, I think, that it is not as if Gogol had a causal sequence in mind and has made the story a kind of rebus or riddle. On the contrary, we sense that even if someone should someday find a principle capable of accounting for this weird sequence of events—say, something in theoretical physics as applied to the physiology of growth and consciousness—the explanation would be wrong even if it did fit, perhaps even because it fit. What we have in "The Nose" is a sequence of "inexplicable phenomena" related inexplicably to each other.

In asking for an explanation of the story, one might also have in mind an allegorical interpretation. However they are caused, what do these events mean? Quite different problems afflict the search for this sort of explanation. As causal explanations are impossible to find, allegorical ones are too easy. Multiple, perhaps infinite, interpretations suggest themselves.

> —Gary Saul Morson, "Gogol's Parables of Explanation: Nonsense and Prosaics." *Essays on Gogol: Logos and the Russian Word.*, eds. Susanne Fusso and Priscilla Meyer. Evanston: Northwestern University Press, 1992: 230.

## DAVID MCDUFF ON VANITY

[David McDuff has translated works by Dostoevsky, Tolstoy, and Babel. In this excerpt, he discusses loss of identity in "The Nose."]

The story gains its uniquely dreamlike quality from the unusual way in which the action is presented. We do not encounter Kovalyov straight away; instead, the opening scene presents, in the style of a newspaper column ("On 25 March there occurred in St. Petersburg an unusually strange event"), the shock received by Kovalyov's barber, Ivan Yakovlevich (his surname has been "lost") on discovering a nose in the roll that has been freshly baked for him by his wife. Seized by fear that the police may arrest him for having cut off the nose of one of his customers while drunk, Ivan Yakovlevich goes out into the streets in order to find some suitable place where he can get rid of the nose. But whenever he tries to drop it or throw it away he is spotted by someone he knows, who invariably tells him that he has dropped something. In the end, he decides to go to Isakievsky Bridge and throw the nose, wrapped in a rag, into the Neva. After he has done this, he is accosted by a surly policeman who refuses to believe his protestations of innocence. At this point the narrative becomes shrouded in mystery: "Of what happened after that, decidedly nothing is known."

The scene now shifts to the quarters of Major Kovalyov. Kovalyov's rank of "collegiate assessor" has been gained not in Russia but in the Caucasus, where such distinctions are more easily acquired, and throughout the story we are made aware of his feelings of unease and inferiority which stem from this fact. The loss of his nose, which he discovers upon taking a mirror to examine a pimple he has had, devastates him, for it attacks him where he is most vulnerable—in his personal vanity. Instead of a nose he has nothing, "a completely smooth place." Gogol places great emphasis on the "nothingness" experienced by Kovalyov. Covering his face with a handkerchief, he sets off immediately to report the loss to the chief of police. On his way he goes into a pastry-cook's shop to examine the "smooth place" again, and coming out of the shop he sees his nose getting out of a carriage. The nose is dressed in the uniform of a very senior civil servant, a councillor of state, and Kovalyov does not at first even dare to approach the august personage. When, in the interior of the Kazan Cathedral, during a religious service, he does accost the nose, it treats him with cold disdain, drawing attention to the great discrepancy in their ranks. After this, it disappears again, and Kovalyov continues on his way to see the chief of police. But the chief is not in his office, and so he goes to the offices of a newspaper in order to place an advertisement requesting the return of his nose. (...)

Like the other St. Petersburg stories, "The Nose" is a semi-comic, semi-tragic meditation on the nature of reality and its inseparable relation to morality. It is Kovalyov's vanity that deprives him, temporarily, of his nose—to him orders, decorations, ranks, and medals are of more account than his own humanity. His moral blindness acquires a life of its own and torments him by fusing with the inhuman, dreamlike environment of the city itself. At one level, Gogol appears to be saying, this is a world in which reality is determined by what is in humans, or missing from them.

—David McDuff, "The Nose: Overview." *Reference Guide to Short Fiction, 1st ed.*, edited by Noelle Watson. Detroit: St. James Press, 1994, 1–2.

# "The Overcoat"

Gogol wrote "The Overcoat" from 1839–1841, but the story was not published until 1842. It supposedly originated from an anecdote Gogol heard about a poor civil servant who desired a hunting rifle, which he obtained by sacrificing and saving, and which he dropped into the water the first time he went duck shooting. Another possible source is a literary one: "The Demon" (1839) by Nikolai Pavlov.

"The Overcoat" has been called the single most famous short story in all of Russian literature. The oft-quoted maxim "We have all come out of Gogol's 'Overcoat,'" which has long been attributed to Dostoevsky, implies that Russian realism in its entirety grew out of this one story. Setchkarev deems it "the most mature, the most perfect among Gogol's shorter narrative works." Nabokov calls it an "immortal" story in which Gogol "became the greatest artist that Russia has yet produced." In addition to this critical acclaim, the story has been debated over by critics of all schools who attempt to appropriate it for their ideological and artistic schemas. What is clear, however, is that the richness in the possibilities of interpretation stems from the inherent richness in the text itself.

"The Overcoat" is the story of a simple St. Petersburg clerk, a titular councillor, named Akaky Akakievich Bashmachkin whose acquisition and loss of a possession, an overcoat, is also a story about humanity and love. The surface plot of "The Overcoat" is about gaining and losing an object, but this is all tied into the subtext of psychological awakening and eroticism. We also see how the anticipation of an object, the coat, and its subsequent obtainment and loss, can profoundly affect the course of one man's life, and also the ramifications it can have on society as a whole.

Two elements of note in "The Overcoat" are the unusual method of narration and the humane passages. The tale is narrated in a colloquial fashion by an omniscient narrator who addresses the reader at points, and who often interrupts the main narration to digress at length on seemingly trivial details about characters. The manner of narration is related to the genre of the *skaz* in which the story is filtered through the unsophisticated consciousness of a narrator who can be characterized as somewhat inept. He places unusual emphasis on irrelevant areas of his narrative and neglects others altogether.

The other important element in the tale is what have been called the "humane passages." The most famous of these is the passage in which Akaky Akakievich fends off the clerks who torment him by asking why they attack him, asserting "I am your brother." It has been interpreted by critics in differing ways. Some say it is meant to inspire pity for Akaky in the reader; others say it is meant to do just the opposite. Some say that the passage shows Gogol's fundamental conviction in the goodness of man and his belief in the Christian brotherhood; others argue that Gogol is emphasizing man's inhumanity to his fellow man. While still others argue that the sentiments expressed represent an unrealized, yet desirable, idealized condition.

The character of Akaky Akakievich Bashmachkin is discussed in extensive detail, right down to the origins of his three names. Critics themselves have probed Gogol's possible reasons for choosing his particular—and peculiar—combination of names. The name "Akaky" has been interpreted many ways. It is the name of the holy martyr St. Acacius, a sixth-century saint famous for his asceticism and his forbearance despite a difficult superior. The name can be said to be derived from the Greek *akakia*, meaning "guilelessness, innocence, simplicity." It has comic overtones, suggesting a child's word for excrement—*kaka*, adding to his pathetic portrait and further reinforcing his "hemorrhoidal" aspect. The name "Akaky Akakievich" can also be a phonetic reference to his habit of stuttering and stammering. His last name, "Bashmachkin" provides further riches. It means "shoe," but since his family members wore boots, the narrator is unclear how the name came about. This adds to the ridiculousness of Akaky, whose name even doesn't seem to fit him. The shoe reference has later relevance, for later, the clerk is described as endeavoring to step as lightly as possible on his tiptoes in order to prevent having to have his shoes resoled.

The narrator succeeds in building up a rich description of the pitiable clerk, both his outer appearance and his inner life. His complexion is even described as "hemorrhoidal." He proceeds throughout life oblivious to everything—flies in his food, garbage tossed at him on the street—except his love for copying documents. This occupation is his only concern and pleasure. Ironically, the clerk is inept with words, yet is obsessed with reproducing them on paper.

Akaky Akakievich aspires to no greater position in his career, which places him squarely outside of the rank-obsessed environment in which he lives. He does not delight in food, social gatherings, or other diversions, but returns home from his days of copying to copy more documents for his own pleasure. He views the world in the context of his "own neat lines." His speech is pitiful, too, for he expresses himself mostly with prepositions, adverbs, and nonsensical particles. All in all, he would have been content to continue on this monotonous path were it not for the disintegration of his overcoat amid the bitterly cold Russian winter.

Akaky begins to feel the cold through his already thin and overly patched overcoat and decides to visit the tailor, Petrovich, to ask him to mend the coat. Some critics have deemed Petrovich to be a manifestation of the devil, pointing to, among other evidence, his deformed toenail and the absence of an eye, both of which are said to signify the devil. The tailor proclaims the old coat beyond hope and says that only a new coat will do. Akaky, on his measly salary of four hundred roubles or thereabouts, despairs when the tailor quotes him with a price of one hundred and fifty roubles. He begs him to repair the coat, but Petrovich stands firm. Akaky leaves, defeated, but with a plan to return Sunday morning when he hopes the tailor will be more amenable. But this, too, is in vain, and Akaky is forced to order a coat, albeit for the much-reduced price of eighty roubles.

In order to save money for the coat, Akaky Akakievich deprives himself of drinking tea in the evening and of burning candles. He forces himself to tread softly on his shoes to avoid wearing out the soles and to take off his clothes upon arriving home to prevent the soling of his linens, thereby sending them to the laundry as infrequently as possible. At first, these changes are a hardship for him, but then he grows accustomed to them; he even goes further in denying himself food in the evening. Rather than disillusioning him, these sacrifices only intensify what he is feeling: an immense never-before-felt sense of purpose. In this way, the ordering of the coat enacts a remarkable change in the clerk. While he loses nourishment from food, he is nourished spiritually by the "eternal" idea of the future coat. The coat replaces his obsession with copying, dominating his life as the latter used to do. His existence loses its one-dimensionality, becoming richer; the idea of the coat is even compared to a spouse. And so the coat comes to represent the concept of love itself. Other remarkable changes occur in his person: he becomes more animated and firmer of character, as doubt and indecision vanish from his face and actions. In addition, he is even excited by the prospect of the coat and muses endlessly about possibilities of material, color, and the like. We see that he has finally acquired what has been missing from his life thus far: a goal.

Upon receiving the coat, he is filled with happiness, both because it is warm and because it represents the fulfillment of his dream. His fellow clerks greet the newly clad Akaky Akakievich with much fanfare, embarrassing the modest clerk. One even goes so far as to announce that he will throw a party in his honor, and he invites everyone for tea that evening. Akaky Akakievich tries to decline, but is unable; he is heartened, though, when he realizes it will give him another opportunity to wear the new coat. He compares the day to that of a "great festive holiday," a happiness which contrasts with the utter despair which follows imminently.

On the way to the party, he notices women for the first time, which is ironic since it is his chaste involvement with the overcoat that has sparked his interest in actual potential love interests. And on his return from the party, he even starts running after a woman. In effect, the overcoat represents love for him, but also his loss of innocence; he is doomed from the moment he desires the object.

The excesses of the party form a marked contrast with the ascetic manner in which Akaky Akakievich is accustomed to spend his evenings. He watches the clerks play cards; he is plied with champagne and rich foods, and finally the sensations prove too much for him and he leaves.

Walking home through the deserted streets, in a joyful state of mind, he is attacked by a gang of men who steal his overcoat. The nearby policeman is of no help, and tells him to go to the inspector the next day to air his grievances. His landlady warns him against the inspector and instead recommends that he see the superintendent. The superintendent only makes things worse, insinuating improprieties on the poor clerk's part for his returning home late from an "indecent" house. Akaky Akakievich is so upset that he misses work that day for the first time ever.

One of Akaky Akakievich's coworkers advises him that he skip going about the police route, and instead, recommends that he visit a certain "important person." Gogol uses this important person as his opportunity to condemn the emphasis placed on rank and the general state of the Russian bureaucracy, which he begins at the very outset of the tale. The important person is a caricature of the worst type of official: one who always feels the need to assert his own significance and superiority in rank. The important person has just been made a general and now finds it impossible to speak to and socialize with those even one rank lower than he. He reprimands the poor clerk for not following the proper procedure, for disregarding the "order" in his circumvention of the usual bureaucratic channels. Akaky Akakievich stutters and stammers, trying in vain to make himself understood. The important person yells at him forcefully, and he faints and is carried out.

Akaky Akakievich walks home through the bitter St. Petersburg winter, through the blizzard and the harsh wind, and promptly becomes ill. He dies, leaving no heirs, possessions, or anyone who cares what happened to him. His life has impacted no one; it is almost as if he never existed. But not quite, for Akaky Akakievich gets his revenge yet. A dead man begins to appear at night in the form of a clerk searching for an overcoat; the man, who pulls overcoats off the shoulders of others, is recognized as none other than Akaky Akakievich. His "noisy" last few days are accounted for as a reward for an entirely "unnoticed" life.

Paradoxically, when he was alive he seemed to be one of the living dead, whereas after death, he shows more life in his actions as a ghost.

The story then shifts to the fate of the important person, who feels remorse over his part in the death of Akaky Akakievich. He tries to take his mind off the matter and cheer himself up by attending a party, with the intention of later visiting his mistress, Karolina Ivanovna. This is not to be, however, for on the way there, he is accosted by the ghost of Akaky Akakievich, who declares his intention of taking the important person's overcoat in return for the latter's failure to help him get his own back. The important person throws off his overcoat and heads for home immediately, all thoughts of his mistress forgotten. The incident has a strong effect on him; he reportedly scolds those officials lower in the hierarchy less often. The ghost also ceases his behavior of throwing people's overcoats off, having found one that fits perfectly. However there are still rumors that a ghost haunts the surrounding areas and bridges of St. Petersburg; it is ambiguous whether this ghost is Akaky Akakievich, the robber who stole Akaky's coat earlier, or some other tortured soul.

# "The Overcoat"

**The Narrator** recounts the tale in a colloquial fashion as an observer omniscient. He addresses the reader at points and often interrupts the main narration to digress at length on seemingly trivial details about characters. This manner of narration is related to the genre of the *skaz* in which the story is filtered through the unsophisticated consciousness of a narrator who can be characterized as somewhat inept. He places unusual emphasis on irrelevant areas of his narrative and neglects others altogether.

**Akaky Akakievich Bashmachkin** is the main character of "The Overcoat." He is a titular councillor, a clerk whose job it is to copy documents endlessly. He is pitiable, both in his physical appearance and in his manner of living and conducting himself. With the promise of a new overcoat, he enjoys a brief elevation in his feelings of happiness, and for the first time in his life, he enjoys a sense of purpose. All this ends when the coat is stolen, and a sequence of events leads to his death. He gets his revenge in the end, however, becoming a ghost who steals coats from others.

**Petrovich** is the tailor who makes the overcoat for Akaky Akakievich. He tells the clerk that his old coat is unfixable, forcing him to order a new one. Critics often consider him to be an incarnation of the devil.

**The Important Person** is the man whom Akaky Akakievich visits, per the advice of a fellow clerk, in order to get his coat back. The important person represents the bureaucratic hierarchy, which Gogol deplored. He has just been made a general, and now finds he cannot associate with anyone even one rank below him. He refuses to help Akaky Akakievich, raging at him for circumventing the usual bureaucratic order in coming to him, thereby directly contributing to the man's death. He is visited by the clerk in death, however, which makes him modify his behavior towards others somewhat.

# CRITICAL VIEWS ON

# "The Overcoat"

## HENRI TROYAT ON REALISM AND SUPERNATURALISM

[Henri Troyat, born in 1911, was a French novelist and biographer of Russian origin whose real name is Lev Tarassov. He is the author of numerous historical novels (including the cycle *Tant que la terre durera*, 1946–48) and biographies of famous Russians, including Tolstoy (1965, tr. 1967), and Ivan the Terrible (1982, tr. 1986). He obtained the Goncourt prize in 1938 for *Araigne*. In *The Divided Soul: The Life of Gogol*, Troyat points out that the apparent break between the realistic part of "The Overcoat" with its supernatural conclusion is not such a division after all.]

Here ends the work of Gogol-the-realist; on the next line begins the work of Gogol-the-ghostly. The phantom of Akaky Akakyevich takes up where the living man left off. (...)

The break between realism and the supernatural is not as sharp as appears at first glance. Even in the more "realistic" part, a swarm of slightly jarring details provide a background of the bizarre. The story of Akaky Akakyevich takes place on two levels. On the surface, we are indeed studying a portrait of an oppressed and humiliated creature colliding with the imbecilic haughtiness of his superiors, and the whole tale can be seen as a satire on Russian bureaucracy or, better still, as a protest against social injustice. But, behind this half-ironic, half-compassionate portrayal of a mini-man with ink-stained fingers, lurks the strange power of the forces of unreason. The nullity of Akaky Akakyevich is such that even in his lifetime he resembles an automaton, a "dead soul."

> —Henri Troyat, *The Divided Soul: The Life of Gogol*, trans. Nancy Amphoux. Garden City, New York: Doubleday & Company, Inc., 1973: 307.

[Boris Eichenbaum (1886–1959) began his career as a medical student but switched to literature, studying and later teaching at St. Petersburg University. His best work was written in the 1920s: *The Melodic Features of Russian Verse* (1922), *The Young Tolstoy* (1923), *Lermontov* (1924), and *Through Literature* (1924). He was prolific, producing a steady output of high-quality scholarly writing throughout a long career, most of it spent in St. Petersburg at the Institute of Russian Literature (Pushkin House) of the Academy of Sciences. During his career, he became a champion of the new Formalist movement, whose principles he applied to the article "How Gogol's 'Overcoat' is Made." Here he relates how Gogol, in "The Overcoat" is able to set up a fictional world where proportions and importance are inverse to those of the real world.]

The thing that Gogol found of value in the story about the clerk was precisely this fantastically limited and self-enclosed complex of thoughts, feelings, and desires, within whose narrow confines the artist is at liberty to exaggerate details and violate the normal proportions of the world. "The Overcoat" is laid out along precisely these lines. The point is certainly not Akaky Akakievich's "insignificance," or a sermon on "humaneness" toward one's lesser brethren, but, rather, Gogol's ability, once he has isolated the entire realm of the story from reality at large, to join together what cannot be joined, to exaggerate what is small and diminish what is great.[29] In a word, he is able to play with all the norms and laws of the inner life as it really is. And this is exactly how he proceeds. Akaky Akakievich's inner world (if in fact such a term is permissible here) is not insignificant (this notion has been introduced by our naive and sentimental historians of literature, who have been mesmerized by Belinsky),[30] but is fantastically limited and his very own: "In his copying he somehow *saw a variegated (!) and pleasant world of his own.*... Outside his copying nothing seemed to exist for him."[31]

This world has its own laws, its own proportions. According to the laws of this world, a new overcoat proves to be a grand event—and Gogol supplies a grotesque formulation: "he did partake of spiritual nourishment, for his thoughts were constantly on the eternal idea of the future overcoat."[32] And again: "It was as if he were no longer alone but were accompanied by some agreeable helpmeet who had consented to walk the road of life with him. This helpmeet was none other than the new overcoat, with its warm padding and its sturdy lining." Small details stand out, such as Petrovich's toenail, which is "thick and hard as a tortoise shell," or his snuff-box "with the portrait of some general or other on it—just which general nobody knew, because the spot where the face used to be had been poked through with a finger and then pasted over with a square piece of paper."

## NOTES

29. "But by a strange order of things, it is always insignificant causes that give rise to great events; and, on the contrary, great undertakings that end in insignificant consequences" ("Old-Fashioned Landowners").

30. See the introduction and the article by Merezhkovsky in the present collection.

31. "The life of their modest owners is so quiet, so very quiet, that for a moment you are lost in forgetfulness and you think that the passions, desires, and disquieting creations of the evil spirit that trouble the world have no existence at all, and that you have seen them only in a glittering, glistening dream" ("Old-Fashioned Landowners"). [The italics and the parenthetical exclamation in the quotation are Eichenbaum's.]

32. In the rough draft, which had not yet been developed into a grotesque, it was put in a different way: "carrying the future overcoat constantly in his thoughts."

—Boris Eichenbaum, "How Gogol's 'Overcoat' is Made." *Gogol from the Twentieth Century: Eleven Essays*, ed. Robert A Maguire. Princeton: Princeton University Press, 1974: 288–289.

## Dmitry Chizhevsky on Diction and the Inanimate Object

[Dmitry Chizhevsky is one of the most versatile and productive researchers and chroniclers of the Slavic world to date. His best-known books in English are *Outline of Comparative Slavic Literatures, On Romanticism in Slavic Literatures,* and *History of Russian Literature from the Eleventh Century to the End of the Baroque.* He has also acted as an editor of Slavic texts, as well as serving as an original and prolific contributor to Gogol studies. In "About 'The Overcoat'" he points out that the impoverishment of the narrator's diction is not accidental, but is in service to the purpose of the story as a whole. Also, he puts forth his view that the theme of "The Overcoat" is the awakening of the soul through the love of an inanimate object.]

The impoverishment of the narrator's diction is therefore no accident. Obviously Gogol was unable to bring it all the way down to the level of the speech of Akaky Akakievich or of the Important Personage. If the narrator had "expressed himself ... in prepositions, adverbs, and, last but not least, in particles of a kind that have absolutely no meaning," or if he had "remained everlastingly in the same taciturn state"—then the result would have been no story at all. However, Gogol does to some degree make his narrator's diction resemble that of his heroes. This is the purpose of the peculiar impoverishment of the language of "The Overcoat." Such impoverishment would seem to contravene the fundamental, intrinsic law of every work of art, which necessarily strives to achieve the greatest possible richness, fullness, and plenitude. But in this case, the possibilities for a richness and fullness of diction are obviously limited by the inarticulateness that is so characteristic of the narrator and the heroes. (...)

The theme of "The Overcoat" is the kindling of the human soul, its rebirth under the influence of love (albeit of a very special kind). It becomes evident that this can happen through contact with any object—not only with one that is grand, exalted, or important (a heroic deed, one's native land, a living human being such as a friend, a beloved woman, etc.), but also with one that is common and ordinary too. As we have seen, the hero's attitude toward the overcoat is depicted in the language of erotic love. And it is not only love for what is grand and important that can destroy a man or pull him down into a bottomless pit; so too can love for an insignificant object, once it has become the object of passion, of love.

> —Dmitry Chizhevsky, "About 'The Overcoat.'" *Gogol from the Twentieth Century: Eleven Essays.*, ed. Robert A. Maguire. Princeton: Princeton University Press, 1974: 300, 315.

## SIMON KARLINSKY ON ALIENATION AND LOVE

[Simon Karlinsky is Professor Emeritus of Slavic Languages and Literatures at the University of California, Berkeley. His current projects include an autobiographical memoir and a study of Chekhov as a Russian playwright. In his work *The Sexual Labyrinth of Nikolai Gogol*, his treatment of "The Overcoat" is particularly illuminating. Karlinsky remarks that "The Overcoat" is noteworthy both for its portrayal of urban alienation and for the way in which Gogol creates sympathy for its main character, Akaky Akakievich, while simultaneously ridiculing him. Here he discusses the interplay between the dangerous nature of love and the injurious implications of change, all with an eye to Gogol's personal views on the social order.]

Sociologically, what is remarkable about "The Overcoat" is not its portrayal of poverty, which was ordinary enough at the time, but its description of urban alienation. It is this aspect of the story that firmly places it within the context of the other stories of the St. Petersburg cycle, written some five years before it. But while the heroes of the other St. Petersburg stories chafe under the burden of loneliness and alienation, the hero of "The Overcoat" seems to have chosen them of his own free will as his natural mode of existence. The real literary triumph of "The Overcoat" is neither the rather obvious sentimentalist episode of the young man who taunts Akaky Akakievich and then realizes with dismay that he has been hurting a fellow human being nor the moving little requiem that Gogol sings after his protagonist's death, but the sympathy the story arouses in the reader for the least human and least prepossessing character in all literature, a man whom the author, furthermore, systematically undercuts and ridicules. (...)

"The Overcoat" is the most perfect artistic embodiment of the two constant, cardinal Gogolian themes: the lethal nature of love and the destructive potential of change—any kind of change. The happiest environments in his work are always the ones in which time stands still and each succeeding generation follows the same familiar and patriarchal mode of existence that the earlier ones did. Such is the world of "Ganz Küchelgarten," of the light opera stories in the Dikanka cycle ("Fair at Sorochintsy," "May Night," "Christmas Eve"), of "Ivan Fyodorovich Shponka and His Aunt" and of "Old-World Landowners." This was also the world inhabited by the protagonists of "Terrible Vengeance," "Taras Bulba," and "Viy" until the intervention of evil forces made a shambles of their well-adjusted lives. In his reclusive, bivalvelike existence, Akaky Akakievich was perfectly adjusted and happy. "It would be hard to find a man whose life was so totally devoted to his work," we are told at the beginning of the story. "To say that he worked with zeal is not enough—no, he worked with love. There, in his copying, he discerned a whole world of his own, varied and agreeable." Fate cannot touch Akaky Akakievich until he becomes involved with his overcoat. Overcoat spells love and love brings on change, and it is at this point that Akaky Akakievich becomes just as vulnerable as the other protagonists of the St. Petersburg cycle of stories. Acquisition of the overcoat takes him out of his routine, out of his own part of town, and even threatens to take him out of the safety of his social isolation. The underlying idea is of course that safety lies only in withdrawal from current life and in lack of action, an essentially ultra-conservative idea that is basic to all of Gogol's social and political thinking. It is odd indeed that the so-called progressive Russian critics, from Belinsky and Chernyshevsky to their present-day self-styled disciples in the Soviet Union, should extol "The Overcoat" and deplore *Selected Passages from Correspondence with Friends* as an incomprehensible aberration on Gogol's part, for the basic philosophical idea of these two works is one and the same: the desirability of total social stasis.

—Simon Karlinsky, *The Sexual Labyrinth of Nikolai Gogol.* Chicago: The University of Chicago Press, 1992: 136–137, 142–143.

## JESSE ZELDIN ON INNOCENCE AND CORRUPTION

[Here, Zeldin states his belief that the events of "The Overcoat" reveal a loss of innocence; the emphasis on materialism corrupts the honesty and integrity of the protagonist, a simple, yet pure, clerk.]

Seldom did Gogol so explicitly speak of the loss of innocence as he did in "The Overcoat." Akaky Akakyevich falls prey to a falsity that destroys him, symbolized by the overcoat and the attitude that he adopts towards it. That overcoat becomes as important to him as his nose did to Kovalyov. It means, and brings, a new life—one like that of other men, unfortunately, for Akaky Akakyevich is accepted; and this, because it is riveted upon the material world—and only the material world—means the loss of innocence. Harmony, beauty, and truth are traded for material deception; integrity is exchanged for appearance in the eyes of others.

—Jesse Zeldin, *Nikolai Gogol's Quest for Beauty: An Exploration into His Works*. Lawrence, KS: The Regents Press of Kansas, 1978: 59.

PLOT SUMMARY OF

# "Ivan Fyodorovich Shponka and His Aunt"

"Ivan Fyodorovich Shponka and His Aunt" is in the second volume (1832) of the two-volume collection of short stories, *Evenings on a Farm near Dikanka*. The story differs from the other seven stories that make up the collection in significant ways. Within the narrative framework of the Dikanka cycle, the other stories are supposedly told by the village beekeeper and his rustic friends, in the oral tradition. These stories depict a fairytalesque Ukraine of the past, and their characters are all peasants or Cossacks. "Ivan Fyodorovich Shponka and His Aunt" is a written work, and one by a man of a higher social class, Stepan Ivanovich Kurochka. It is set in the present, portrays Ukrainian gentry, and contains no magical or supernatural elements. For these reasons, the story is also notable for delineating a turning point in Gogol's literary development, especially with regard to his contribution to realism. The story is even said to contain the attributes of the style that were to characterize Gogol's later masterpieces.

"Ivan Fyodorovich Shponka and His Aunt" is composed of six sections, five titled and one untitled introductory passage. In the introduction, a narrator, Rudy Panko, the beekeeper (from previous tales), informs us that the story he is about to relate was told to him by Stepan Ivanovich Kurochka, who later transcribed it for the narrator. In this way, the introduction connects the story with the others by means of the figure of Panko, while it also separates it from the others by making another narrator the author. Unfortunately, though, the narrator's wife used the paper on which the story was written to make pastries. Thus, only part of the tale survives. The fact that the narrator tries to track down Stepan Ivanovich for the missing part of the story and that he urges the reader to do the same if in the man's neighborhood, heightens the reader's anticipation for the account that will follow.

"Ivan Fyodorovich Shponka and His Aunt" is the story of a man named Ivan Fyodorovich Shponka, who, urged by his aunt, retires from the army, to return to his family estate. Ostensibly, the purpose of his homecoming is to help his aging aunt manage the estate, but she has an ulterior motive in requesting his presence. The name "Shponka," which means dowel (a type of tool), is an apt one for Ivan, for he is a tool that his aunt wields to enact her plan. From the moment that he agrees to come home, she has him firmly in her power.

## I. Ivan Fyodorovich Shponka

The narrator gives us background on Ivan Fyodorovich including his character as a child. He was very meticulous, neat, systematic, and well behaved. The narrator relates one particular anecdote that had a far-reaching effect on the course of Ivan Fyodorovich's life. One of the students whom he had as a class monitor brought him a pancake to bribe Ivan to mark that the boy knew his Latin lesson when, in fact, he was unprepared. Ivan was hungry at that moment and unable to resist temptation; he took the pancake and began to eat. Just then, the terrible Latin teacher came in, threw the pancake out the window, and beat Ivan very badly on the hands. Ivan's timidity, already great, increased even more. The writer of the tale speculates that this incident might be the reason why Ivan never wanted to enter the civil service. It also foreshadows—and explains—an incident that will occur later in Ivan's terrible dream.

At age seventeen, he joined the P—— infantry regiment. This boisterous regiment, filled with men who enjoyed drinking and gambling on their off hours, did not lessen his shyness. While his fellow soldiers went out carousing, Ivan sat at home and occupied himself with such humble tasks as polishing buttons and setting mousetraps. Ivan Fyodorovich brought the same sense of discipline to commanding his platoon that he employed in conducting himself in his daily life. In fact, he was so successful that in a short time, eleven years after being made ensign, he was promoted to sub-lieutenant.

Shortly after being promoted, Ivan Fyodorovich learns that his mother has died and that her sister, his aunt, whom he does not know well, has taken over the small estate to manage it for him. Ivan is content to let her do this, and goes about his business as if nothing has changed. Four years later, however, his aunt Vasilisa Kashporovna sends him a letter informing him that she can no longer look after the estate on her own and that it is time for him to manage it. She also mentions that she has something to reveal to him. Ivan sends her back a letter saying that he is resigning and will be there soon. He hires a Jew to take him to the estate in Gadyach.

## II. THE ROAD

After two weeks of travelling, they come to a village about seventy miles from Gadyach where they stay in an inn. There he meets a man named Grigory Grigorievich Storchenko, who, upon hearing where Ivan is headed, tells him that he lives in the same Gadyach district, in the village of Khortyshche, about four miles from Ivan's estate Vytrebenki. He is an ostentatious and overbearing man, who orders his servant around and pressures Ivan into having a drink of cordial with him at the inn. Grigory Grigorievich urges Ivan to visit him at his home once he arrives at his estate; the next day, he is gone.

Three days later, Ivan Fyodorovich arrives at his farmstead. Upon seeing the place, he remembers events from his youth that occurred there, and he reminisces. He is surprised at how robust his aunt is after her communication of her ill health and feebleness to him in her letter. He does not realize that his assistance in managing the estate is not the real reason she has summoned him.

## III. THE AUNT

The narrator then launches into a description of Aunt Vasilisa Kashporovna. She, a woman of fifty, has never been married, which he ascribes to the fact that she causes men to become cowardly in her presence. It is almost as if she and the men who are near her reverse their traditional gender roles. Her appearance is even manly: she is tall, has a large build, and is very strong. She even engages in masculine activities: she rows boats, hunts, climbs trees, beats vassals, and the like. Vasilisa Kashporovna also supervised the kitchen and everything else on the estate, and Ivan finds a flourishing estate when he arrives.

Ivan turns out to be an equally adept manager of the estate, and the farm even brings him joy. His prowess makes his aunt very happy, and she often boasts of his ability in this realm. One day, she informs him that his land extends beyond where he thought the boundary was located. She asks him if he remembers a man named Stepan Kuzmich, who used to visit his mother when Ivan's father was not at home. This man owned all the land beyond Ivan's farmstead and even the village of Khortyshche itself. It is hinted that Stepan Kuzmich is Ivan's real father, and according to the aunt, he left Ivan the deed to fifty acres of land. She tells him that she doesn't know what his mother had done with the deed, but that she thinks Grigory Grigorievich Storchenko, who got possession of the whole estate, has concealed it. Ivan tells her of his coincidental encounter with that man at the inn, and he agrees, upon his aunt's urging, to visit him with the express purpose of trying to recover the deed.

## IV. THE DINNER

Ivan Fyodorovich arrives at Grigory Grigorievich's estate at dinnertime. Ivan makes clear that he is there on business, but his host has ideas of a longer visit. Ivan decides, despite his shyness, to act aggressively, and he mentions Stepan Kuzmich's deed. Grigory is extremely displeased by this mention, first pretending to have trouble hearing and then insisting that the aunt's words are lies. He contends that his uncle never made such a gift, for although the deed is mentioned in the will, it has never been found. Ivan considers that his aunt might have imagined the situation.

Grigory Grigorievich coerces Ivan into having dinner with him, his mother, and his two sisters. There is another guest present, Ivan Ivanovich, who says he remembers Ivan

Fyodorovich from when he was a young boy, as well as his father and his memorable melons. They all sit at the dining room table, and a comical scene follows. An example of the ridiculousness of this dinner scene is a debate that ensues over what part of the turkey Ivan Fyodorovich should eat.

After dinner, Grigory Grigorievich leaves for his room, and everyone else repairs to the living room. Free from the overbearing man, the hostess, his mother, becomes more talkative, and so do the sisters; the younger, prettier one, though, is quieter. Ivan Ivanovich talks most of all, an example of the type of man who relishes conversation and who will talk about any topic. Ivan Fyodorovich, despite attempts to get him to stay the night, manages to leave eventually.

### V. THE AUNT'S NEW PLOT

Vasilisa Kashporovna greets Ivan on his return with inquiries about the success of his mission. When Ivan tells her that Grigory Grigorievich does not have any deed, she asserts that he is lying, but then she changes the subject completely with questions about the dinner. Ivan mentions the younger sister's beauty, and an idea is kindled in his aunt's mind—an alternate method of retrieving the land. She inquires about the woman's beauty, her clothing, whether she and Ivan conversed. Ivan realizes that his aunt is trying to gauge the woman's suitability for becoming his wife as well as his interest in a situation of that kind. He conveys his displeasure in the future of such a state of affairs. In spite of her nephew's reaction, Vasilisa Kashporovna keeps the dream of little grandchildren and a wedding in her mind, and becomes preoccupied with these fantasies. Perhaps she longs for Ivan to be settled, but it seems more likely that she views the possibility of an alliance as a way to resolve the land dispute.

Four days later, Ivan Fyodorovich and his aunt go to visit the estate of Grigory Grigorievich, who is not at home. Vasilisa Kashporovna greets his mother with great deference and thanks her for her hospitality towards her nephew. They—including the two daughters—proceed to settle in the living room where the aunt and the old hostess become engaged in animated conversation. It appears as if they have known each other for a long time, and Vasilisa Kashporovna speaks in such a soft voice to the old lady that Ivan cannot decipher what is being said.

When the old lady arises, ostensibly to show the aunt something, the two girls also get up. The aunt motions to Ivan to stay and says something to the old lady. She, in turn, orders the fair daughter "Mashenka" to keep Ivan company. An extremely awkward scene ensues in which both of them sit silently. Ivan, in his acute discomfort, musters up enough courage to comment on the abundance of flies in the summer, to which the fair lady replies that her brother made a fly swatter out of an old shoe, but that that did not seem to improve their profusion. She and Ivan's conversation ceases, and they are saved by the return of the aunt, the old lady, and the older sister.

On the way back to their estate, Vasilisa Kashporovna launches into a lecture on the necessity of Ivan's having children and a wife. Ivan responds that he would not know "what to do" with a wife. She tells him that he will not find a better wife than Marya Grigorievna and that she has already discussed the matter with the old lady, who would be pleased to have him as her son-in-law. This plan makes Ivan break out into a sweat as he thinks fearfully of the strangeness of living with a wife. It seems as if Ivan's fear of women is motivated by a fear of the unknown and the incomprehensible more than anything else.

That night, Ivan has frightful, incoherent nightmares that can be thought of as surreal. They are filled with the protean image of a wife that surfaces in every conceivable place. First, he dreams that someone grabs him by the ear, saying it is his wife. Then he dreams that he is married to someone and does not know what to say to her; she has a goose face. He turns and sees another wife, also with a goose face. The wives begin to multiply rapidly: he takes off his hat, and finds another wife; he reaches into his pocket and finds another; he takes cotton out of his ear and finds another. He begins to hop on one foot, and his aunt tells him he must hop because he is a married man. The aunt morphs into a belfry, and Ivan feels like someone is pulling him on a rope up the belfry. Ivan tries to assert himself, insisting that he is not a bell, but his efforts are futile. The colonel of the P—— infantry regiment, surfacing from his past, insists that he is one. Then he dreams that his wife is some kind of woolen fabric which he gets in a shop and which the tailor will not make into a coat because it is poor fabric.

Ivan Fyodorovich wakes up in a cold sweat. The ever-shifting form of the wife that appears everywhere has the effect of making him feel as if escape from the fate of marriage is impossible. The dream, while communicating his fear of marriage, also encapsulates the personality traits that Ivan has displayed throughout his life: timidity and passivity. In addition, the dream has an added element of terror and grotesqueness if Ivan and Marya are indeed related, as they would be if Ivan's father really were Stepan Kuzmich. In the morning, Ivan consults his tattered fortune-telling book, but cannot find a suitable interpretation of his dream.

The story abruptly ends with the narrator's informing us that a new plot has been brewing in the aunt's mind, which the reader will learn about in the next chapter. This chapter and the ones to follow have presumably been used by Panko's wife to make pastries, so the true ending is never revealed. This has the effect of both fracturing and fragmenting the narrative, as well as shrouding the entire story in an air of mystery.

# "Ivan Fyodorovich Shponka and His Aunt"

**Ivan Fyodorovich Shponka** is the main character of the tale. Although he is thirty-eight years old, he is very naïve and childish. He is both extremely timid and passive. This latter quality makes his name, "Shponka," particularly apt, for it means "dowel," a type of tool. Indeed, his aunt uses Ivan as a tool in her elaborate plot to regain the land that she feels has been unfairly denied to the family's estate. Ivan has as many feminine characteristics as his aunt has masculine.

**Vasilisa Kashporovna** is Ivan Fyodorovich's aunt, the sister of his late mother. With her masculine physical features and her behavior, as well as her prowess in the kitchen, she acts as both a patriarchal and matriarchal figure for Ivan. She is a calculating woman, who is bent on settling the land dispute between her and her neighbor Grigory Grigorievich Storchenko by orchestrating a marriage between his sister and her nephew.

**Grigory Grigorievich Storchenko** is a loud, forceful, and pompous man. He lives in the Gadyach district, in the village of Khortyshche, about four miles from Ivan's estate Vytrebenki. He denies knowing anything about the deed his uncle allegedly gave Ivan's mother.

**Marya Grigorievna ("Mashenka")** is the sister of Grigory Grigorievich Storchenko and at age twenty-five, she is the youngest of the two daughters of the old lady. She is described as being fair-haired and beautiful. She shares Ivan Fyodorovich's characteristics of shyness and social awkwardness, which makes their interaction with each other painfully difficult.

**Ivan Ivanovich** is a friend of Grigory Grigorievich Storchenko. He attends a dinner party at the Storchenko's where he tries to engage Ivan Fyodorovich in conversation to no avail. He delights in the act of talking and, given the opportunity, will ramble on aimlessly on any topic.

**Stepan Ivanovich Kurochka** is the man who transcribed the tale of Ivan Fyodorovich for the beekeeper Rudy Panko, who is the narrator of the other stories in the collection, *Evenings on a Farm near Dikanka*. The reader is invited to call on him if passing through Gadyach to procure the rest of the Ivan story, which was inadvertently destroyed by Rudy's wife. One of his most marked characteristics is his habit of waving his arms when he walks, resembling a windmill.

# "Ivan Fyodorovich Shponka and His Aunt"

## LEONARD J. KENT ON THE FEAR OF WOMEN

[Here, Kent shows how Ivan's dream in "Ivan Fyodorovich Shponka and His Aunt" reveals his fear of women.]

Even on its most elemental level, the dream accomplishes a profound change in our views of Špon ka. It indicates that he is less naive than he is afraid of women and marriage; there is a soul beneath the gross, impenetrable exterior. Women will force him to do what he does not want to do; they will obligate him, make him hop on one leg. They will complicate his sweet existence, force him out of himself, make him expose himself.

—Leonard J. Kent, *The Subconscious in Gogol' and Dostoevskij, and its Antecedents.* The Hague: Mouton & Co., 1969: 72.

## JAMES B. WOODWARD ON THE DREAM AS ASSAULT

[James B. Woodward is the author of *Russian Literature and the Russian Language Literature* (1981). In this excerpt, he discusses the symbolism of the female specters in Shponka's dream.]

But the story of Storchenko is now discontinued. Its end is prefigured and its role is exhausted—namely, that of proclaiming that under the combined assault of swotter, heat and shoe even the most masculine of males is doomed to succumb. It remains only to convey the pain of final submission as now experienced by the impotent hero, and this is achieved in the concluding two pages by evoking the female invasion of his disintegrating mind. The process commences with his bombardment by "noise". When the sentence of marriage is duly confirmed, "Ivan

Fyodorovich," we read, "stood as though deafened by thunder" (306), and yet again we are reminded of Chichikov's arrival at Korobochka's estate—of the claps of thunder, the barking hounds and the stunning clock which in rapid succession assail his ears (VI, 44–6). In both cases noise seems to symbolise the female assault on the male's senses and vitalit[22] and thus motivates the transition to the motif of sleep which is used, as we have noted, to mark Storchenko's weakening. While Chichikov feels that "his eyes had stuck, as if someone had smeared them with honey" (VI, 45) and immediately retires to the bed that awaits him, Shpon'ka, we are told, "went to bed earlier than usual" (307).[23]

But whereas Chichikov is blissfully unaware of his perilous position and consequently lapses into peaceful repose the sleep of Shpon'ka is rent by female spectres. From every side in the world of his dreams, while "everything around him was whirling with noise", he is assailed by "wives" in bizarre disguises, and prominent among them is logically his aunt—the arbiter of his fate and embodiment of his conception of the female personality. Here the device of dream is used by Gogol both to associate the notion of a wife with the masculine persecutors of Shpon'ka's personal experience—not only with Vasilisa Kashporovna, but also with his regimental colonel and the Latin master who, like one of the "wives", once "seized him by the ear" (285, 307)—and also to generate new metaphors of the masculinized female (...)

NOTES

22. See *GDS*, pp 80–81.

23. In general, the motif of sleep plays an important part in the tale in conveying Shpon'ka's lack of masculine vitality. Thus even during his army career, the narrator discloses, he was given to "lying on his bed" (286), and perhaps another variation of the motif, designed to convey his passivity on his first meeting with Storchenko, may be perceived in the reference to the pleasure that he derives from kissing the latter's "large cheeks" which "felt to his lips like soft pillows" (290).

—James B. Woodward, *The Symbolic Art of Gogol: Essays on his Short Fiction*. Slavica Publishers, Inc., 1981: 32.

# MICHAEL R. KATZ ON THE REAL AND SURREAL

[Michael R. Katz is a Professor of Russian, and Dean of Language Schools and Schools Abroad at Middlebury College, having taught previously at Williams College and the University of Texas at Austin. He is the author of a number of annotated translations including works by Tolstoy, Dostoevsky, and Turgenev, as well as numerous critical articles. He has published two critical books, *The Literary Ballad in Early Nineteenth-Century Russian Literature* and *Dreams and the Unconscious in Nineteenth-century Russian Fiction*. In this excerpt from the latter, he shows how the seeming-reality of "Ivan Fyodorovich Shponka and His Aunt" is disturbed by its surreal conclusion.]

But this seemingly realistic story unexpectedly concludes with a surrealistic nightmare. In it, many of the stylistic devices characteristic of the mature Gogol are previewed: people are transformed into things; images duplicate and proliferate; bizarre hyperboles, hypnotic repetitions, and illogical propositions predominate. Shponka's dream undermines the realism of the preceding narrative and demonstrates that the surface reality of Gogol's world is only apparent. Genuine reality is revealed through the chaos of the hero's nightmare. Albrecht Dürer once gave some advice to his fellow artists: "If a person wants to create the stuff that dreams are made of, let him mix freely all sorts of creatures."[14] This is precisely what Gogol does in Shponka's fantastic dream.

NOTE

14. Quoted in W. Kayser, *The Grotesque in Art and Literature* (Bloomington, Ind., 1963), 21–22.

> —Michael R. Katz, *Dreams and the Unconscious in Nineteenth-century Russian Fiction*. Hanover, NH: University Press of New England, 1984: 76.

## DANIEL RANCOUR-LAFERRIERE ON PSYCHOANALYSIS AND THE DREAM

[Daniel Rancour-Laferriere is Professor of Russian and Director of the Russian program at the University of California-Davis. He has published extensively on Russian history and literature, including *Out From Under Gogol's Overcoat: A Psychoanalytic Study* (1982). In this excerpt, he discusses "Shponka" from a Freudian perspective.]

Just before Špon′ka goes to bed and has his dream he is told by his "auntie" that it is high time for him to marry: "Pora podumat′ ... ob detjax! Tebe nepremenno nužna žena ..." (306). Špon′ka, the epitome of Gogolian "nevinnost′" (Ermilov, 119 ff.), is completely taken aback by this idea. The thirty-eight-year-old bachelor declares that, since he has never been married before, he wouldn't know what to do with a wife ("Ja soveršenno ne znaju, čto s neju delat′!," 306). But the auntie is unfazed by this little Gogolian alogism (to use Slonimskij's term). She insists on a marriage, and Špon′ka begins to feel terrified: "... ženit′sja! ... èto kazalos′ emu tak stranno, tak čudno, čto on nikak ne mog podumat′ bez straxa. Žit′ s ženoju! ... ne ponjatno! On ne odin budet v svoej komnate, no ix dolžno byt′ vezde dvoe! ..." (306-7). It never occurs to Špon′ka that he is not obliged to follow his auntie's orders.

A few lines later Špon′ka is asleep and is dreaming that he is already married. One of the first images to appear in the dream is a double bed—not the single bed he has been used to in the past: "... v ego komnate stoit, vmesto odinokoj, dvojnaja krovat′." This double/single idea had, however, already been on Špon′ka's mind just before the dream, as we have seen ("On ne odin budet v svoej komnate, no ix dolžno byt′ vezde dvoe!"). Thus, there is a subtext for a portion of the dream text in the previous text. This is to be expected since, as Freud showed in *The Interpretation of Dreams*, bits and pieces of what is dreamt can usually be traced to previous perceptual experiences of the dreamer. The many critics who have found fragments of Špon′ka's previous experiences in his dream merely confirm one of the commonplaces of psychoanalysis.

Whereas before the dream Šponʹka was thinking he would now have to go everywhere in life with a wife ("vezde dvoe"), in the dream his attention shifts to one specific place where he must now be with his wife, i.e., in the conjugal bed ("dvojnaja krovatʹ"). It doesn't take a psychoanalyst to see this. The opening portion of the dream text effects a semantic transition from general matters to sexual matters. There is also a semantic effect on the remainder of the dream. If the dream begins with an overt reference to conjugal sexuality, then the remainder of the dream can develop this theme. One would expect the remainder of the dream to be affected in some way by its opening.

—Daniel Rancour-Laferriere, "Šponʹka's Dream Interpreted." *Slavic and East European Journal*, 33, no. 1 (1989): 359–360.

# Nikolai Gogol

## POETRY

*Hans Kuechelgarten*, 1829.
*Italy* (attributed), 1829.

## FICTION

*The Hetman* (one chapter from the projected novel, never completed), 1830–32
*Evenings on a Farm near Dikanka*, Part I, 1831.
*Evenings on a Farm near Dikanka*, Part II, 1832.
*Arabesques*, 1835.
*Mirgorod*, Part I, 1835.
*The Carriage*, 1836.
*The Nose*, 1836.
*Dead Souls*, Part I, 1842.
*The Overcoat*, 1842.
*The Portrait* (revised), 1842.
*Taras Bulba* (revised), 1842.
*Rome*, 1842.

## PLAYS

*The Order of St. Vladimir, Third Class*, 1832–1834.
*The Inspector General*, 1836.
*Marriage*, 1842.
*The Gamblers*, 1842.
*Leaving the Theater After the Performance of a New Comedy*, 1842.

## NONFICTION

"Woman," 1830.

*Arabesques*, 1835

*Petersburg Notes of 1836*, 1837.

*The Petersburg Stage in 1835–36*, 1837.

*A Textbook of Literature for Russian Youth*, written 1844–45, 1896.

*Meditations on the Divine Liturgy*, written 1845–47, 1857.

Denouement of the *Inspector General*, written 1846, 1856.

Second Edition of the Ending of the Denouement of "The *Inspector General.*" 1846.

Foreword to the second edition [of *Dead Souls*]. "To the Reader from the Author," 1846.

On *The Contemporary*, written 1846, 1857.

Forewarning for Those Who Would Like to Play *The Inspector General* Properly, written 1846, 1886.

*Selected Passages from Correspondence with Friends*, 1847.


## MISCELLANEOUS

*A Book of Odds and Ends, or A Handy Encyclopedia*, written 1826–27, 1952.

*Notes Toward a Plan for Touring Rome, for A.O. Smirnova*, written 1843, 1898.

*Notebook for 1841–1844*, written 1841–1844, 1951.

*Notebook for 1846*, written, 1846 1952.

Materials for a Dictionary of the Russian Language, written 1848–51, 1891.

WORKS ABOUT

# Nikolai Gogol

Debreczeny, Paul. *Nikolay Gogol and his Contemporary Critics.* Transactions of the American Philosophical Society. Vol. 56 [n.s], Part 3. Philadelphia: The American Philosophical Society, 1966.

Driessen, F.C. *Gogol as a Short-Story Writer: A Study of His Technique of Composition.* Trans. Ian F. Finley. The Hague: Mouton & Co., 1965.

Erlich, Victor. *Gogol.* New Haven: Yale University Press, 1969.

Fanger, Donald. *The Creation of Nikolai Gogol.* Cambridge, MA: Harvard University Press, 1979.

Fusso, Susanne and Priscilla Meyer, eds. *Essays on Gogol: Logos and the Russian Word.* Evanston: Northwestern University Press, 1992.

Gippius, V.V., *Gogol.*, ed. Trans. Robert A. Maguire. Ann Arbor: Ardis, 1981.

Gogol, Nikolai. *Letters of Nikolai Gogol.* Ed., Carl R. Proffer. Trans. Carl R. Proffer in collaboration with Vera Krivoshein. Ann Arbor: The University of Michigan Press, 1967.

Graffy, Julian. *Gogol's "The Overcoat."* London: Bristol Classical Press, 2000.

Grayson, Jane and Faith Wigzell, eds. *Nicolay Gogol: Text and Context.* London: The Macmillan Press Ltd., 1989.

Herman, David. *Poverty of the Imagination: Nineteenth-Century Russian Literature about the Poor.* Evanston, IN: Northwestern University Press, 2001.

Hingley, Ronald. *Russian Writers and Society, 1825–1904.* New York: McGraw-Hill Book Company, 1967.

Karlinsky, Simon. *The Sexual Labyrinth of Nikolai Gogol.* Chicago: The University of Chicago Press, 1992.

Katz, Michael R. *Dreams and the Unconscious in Nineteenth-century Russian Fiction.* Hanover, New Hampshire: University Press of New England, 1984.

Kent, Leonard J. *The Subconscious in Gogol' and Dostoevskij, and its Antecedents*. The Hague: Mouton & Co., 1969.

Lavrin, Janko. *Nikolai Gogol: A Centenary Survey (1809–1852)*. New York: Russell & Russell, 1968.

Lindstrom, Thais. *Nikolay Gogol*. New York: Twayne Publishers, 1974.

Magarshack, David. *Gogol: A Life*. New York: Grove Press, 1957.

Maguire, Robert A. *Exploring Gogol*. Stanford: Stanford University Press, 1994.

———, ed. and trans. *Gogol from the Twentieth Century: Eleven Essays*. Princeton: Princeton University Press, 1974.

Moeller-Sally, Stephen. *Gogol's Afterlife: The Evolution of a Classic in Imperial and Soviet Russia*. Evanston: Northwestern University Press, 2002.

Moser, Charles A, ed. *The Russian Short Story: A Critical History*. Boston: G.K. Hall & Co., 1986.

Nabakov, Vladimir. *Nikolai Gogol*. New York: New Directions, 1944.

Peace, Richard A. *The Enigma of Gogol: An Examination of the Writings of N.V. Gogol and Their Place in the Russian Literary Tradition*. New York: Cambridge University Press, 1981.

Rancour-Laferriere, Daniel. *Out from Under Gogol's Overcoat: A Psychoanalytic Study*. Ann Arbor: Ardis, 1982.

Rowe, William Woodin. *Through Gogol's Looking Glass: Reverse Vision, False Focus, and Precarious Logic*. New York: New York University Press, 1976.

Shapiro, Gavriel. *Nikolai Gogol and the Baroque Cultural Heritage*. University Park, Pennsylvania: The Pennsylvania University Press, 1993.

Setchkarev, Vsevolod. *Gogol—His Life and Works*. New York: New York University Press, 1965.

Spieker, Sven, ed. *Gogol: Exploring Absence: Negativity in 19th-Century Russian Literature*. Bloomington, IN: Slavica Publishers, Inc., 1999.

Trahan, Elizabeth, ed. *Gogol's "Overcoat": An Anthology of Critical Essays*. Ann Arbor: Ardis, 1982.

Troyat, Henri. *The Divided Soul: The Life of Gogol*. Trans. Nancy Amphoux. Garden City, New York: Doubleday & Company, Inc., 1973.

Vinogradov, V.V. *Gogol and the Natural School*. Ann Arbor: Ardis, 1987.

Waszink, P.M. *"Such Things Happen in the World": Deixis in Three Short Stories by N.V. Gogol*. Amsterdam: Rodopi, 1988.

Woodward, James B. *The Symbolic Art of Gogol: Essays on His Short Fiction*. Columbus, OH: Slavica Publishers, Inc., 1982.

Worrall, Nick. *Nikolai Gogol and Ivan Turgenev*. London: The Macmillan Press Ltd., 1982.

Zeldin, Jesse. *Nikolai Gogol's Quest for Beauty: An Exploration into His Works*. Lawrence, Kansas: The Regents Press of Kansas, 1978.

# ACKNOWLEDGMENTS

*The Subconscious in Gogol' and Dostoevskij, and its Antecedents* by Leonard J. Kent. The Hague: Mouton & Co. (1969): 72, 76, 83–84. © 1969 by Mouton and Co. Reprinted by permission.

*The Creation of Nikolai Gogol* by Donald Fanger. Cambridge: The Belknap Press of Harvard University Press (1979): 113–115. © 1979 by the President and Fellows of Harvard College. Reprinted by permission.

"Gogol's 'The Portrait,': The Simultaneity of Madness, Naturalism, and the Supernatural" by Robert Louis Jackson. From *Essays on Gogol: Logos and the Russian World*, edited by Susanne Fusso and Priscilla Meyer. Evanston: Northwestern University Press, 1992: 106, 111. © 1992 by Northwestern University Press. Reprinted by permission.

"The Devils in the Details: The Role of Evil in the Short Fiction of Nikolai Vasilievich Gogol and Nathaniel Hawthorne" by Derek Maus. From *Papers on Languages & Literature* 38, no. 1 (Winter 2002): 91–92. © 2002 by Southern Illinois University Press. Reprinted by permission.

*Nikolai Gogol's Quest for Beauty: An Exploration into His Works* by Jesse Zeldin. Lawrence, KS: The Regents Press of Kansas (1978): 40, 52, 59. © 1978 by The Regents Press of Kansas. Reprinted by permission.

From *Gogol* by Vasily V. Gippius, ed. and trans. Robert A. Maguire. Ann Arbor: Ardis, (1981): 50. © 1981 by Overlook Press. Reprinted by permission.

*The Enigma of Gogol: An Examination of the Writings of N.V. Gogol and Their Place in the Russian Literary Tradition* by Richard Peace. New York: Cambridge University Press, 1981: 98, 102–103, 104–105. © 1981 by Cambridge University Press. Reprinted with the permission of Cambridge University Press.

*Nikolai Gogol and the Baroque Cultural Heritage* by Gavriel Shapiro. University Park, PA: The Pennsylvania State University Press, 1993: 202. © 1993 by The Pennsylvania State University Press. Reprinted by permission.

"The Nose" by Ivan Yermakov. From *Gogol from the Twentieth Century: Eleven Essays*, edited by Robert A. Maguire. Princeton: Princeton University Press (1974): 195, 197. © 1974 by Princeton University Press. Reprinted by permission of Princeton University Press.

"Gogol's 'The Nose' or the Devil in the Works" by Ann Shukman. From *Nicolay Gogol: Text and Context*. London: The Macmillan Press Ltd. (1989): 66–67. © 1989 by Palgrave Macmillan. Reprinted by permission.

"Gogol's Parables of Explanation: Nonsense and Prosaics" by Gary Saul Morson. From *Essays on Gogol: Logos and the Russian Word*, edited by Susanne Fusso and Pricilla Meyer. Evanston: Northwestern University Press, 1992: 230. © 1992 by Northwestern University Press. Reprinted by permission.

"The Nose: Overview" by David McDuff. From *Reference Guide to Short Fiction, 1st ed.*, edited by Noelle Watson. Detroit: St. James Press, 1994: 1–2. © 1994 by St. James Press. Reprinted by permission of the Gale Group.

*The Divided Soul: The Life of Gogol* by Henri Troyat. Trans. Nancy Amphoux. Garden City, New York: Doubleday & Company, Inc., 1973: 307. © 1973 by Random House Inc. Reprinted by permission.

"How Gogol's 'Overcoat' is Made" by Boris Eichenbaum. From *Gogol from the Twentieth Century: Eleven Essays*, edited by Robert A. Maguire. Princeton: Princeton University Press, 1974: 288–289. © 1974 by Princeton University Press. Reprinted by permission of Princeton University Press.

"About 'The Overcoat" by Dmitry Chizhevsky. From *Gogol from the Twentieth Century: Eleven Essays*, edited by Robert A. Maguire. Princeton: Princeton University Press, 1974: 300,

# Themes and Ideas